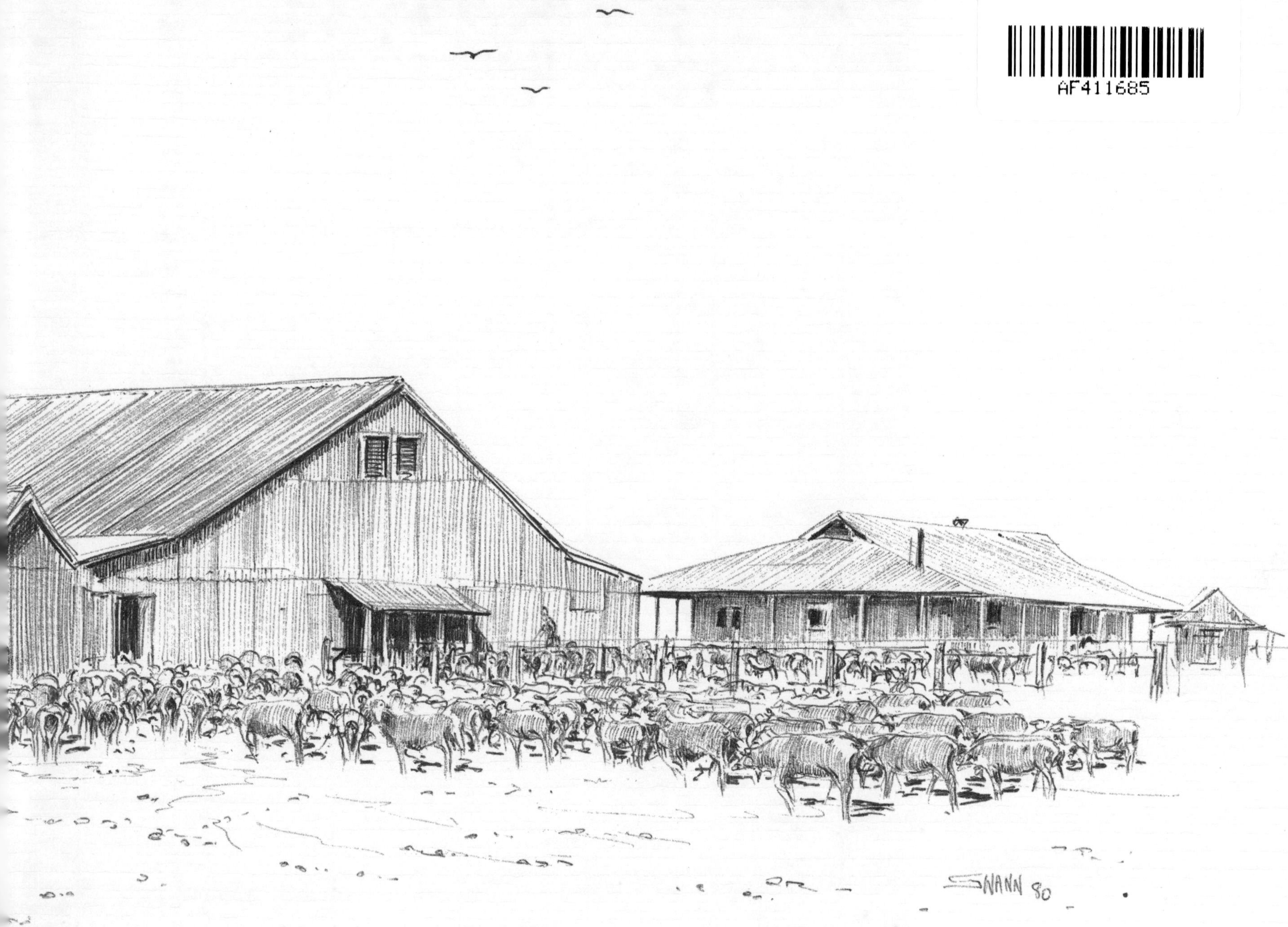

Janet and James M. Prouley——

October, 19 0

Adelaide, South Australia

Images of
South Australia

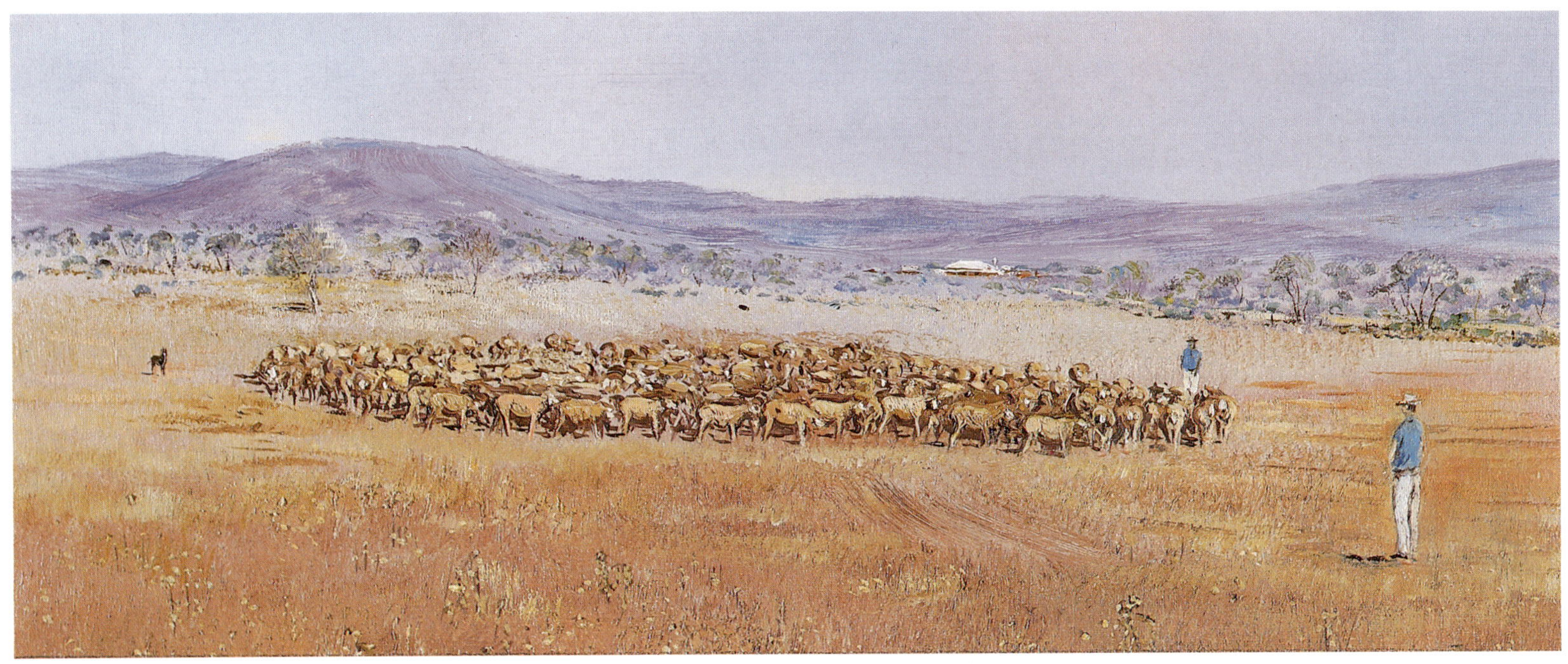

By the same artist:

SWANN'S SOUTH AUSTRALIA
SWANN 71
SWANN BEYOND THE DARLING
UNIVERSITY OF ADELAIDE—DRAWINGS
SOUTH AUSTRALIA WITH SWANN
SWANN AT HOME AND ABROAD
SWANN'S AUSTRALIA

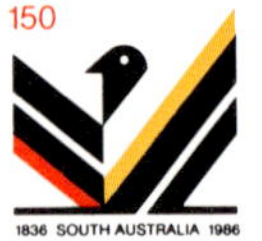

A South Australian Jubilee 150 publication.

The Wakefield Press has been established by
the Government and is funded by the Jubilee
150 Board of South Australia.

Images of
South Australia

BRUCE SWANN

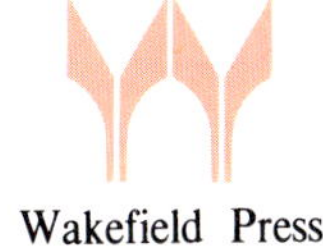

Wakefield Press

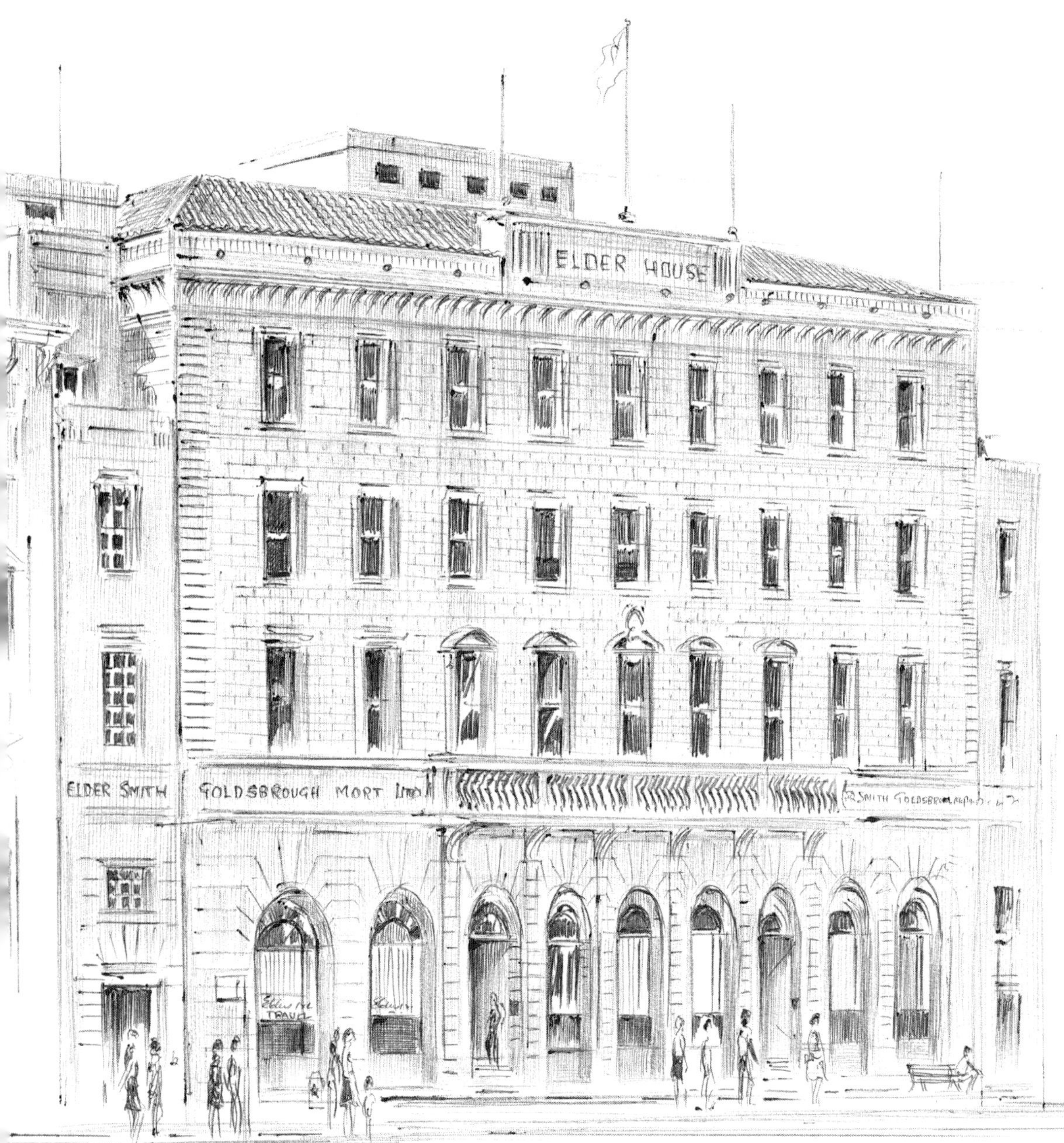

Elder House, Currie Street, Adelaide

First published 1985
Wakefield Press
282 Richmond Road
NETLEY SA 5037

National Library of Australia
Cataloguing-in-publication entry

Swann, Bruce, 1925-
    Images of South Australia.

    ISBN 0 949268 34 8.
    ISBN 0 949268 33 X (de luxe).

    1. Swann, Bruce, 1925- . 2. Landscape painting,
    Australian—South Australia. 3. South Australia in art.
    4. Drawing, Australian. I. Title.

759.994

Wholly set-up and produced in Adelaide, South Australia
Design: Con Tsitsinaris • Photo typesetting: Delmonts Pty Ltd
Printing: Stock Journal Publishers Pty Ltd • Binding: Advance
Bookbinders Pty Ltd

FOREWORD

The release of *Images of South Australia* was planned to help celebrate South Australia's Jubilee 150. Although the images do include scenes of sea and city, I suppose it is only natural that a good many of the illustrations feature woolsheds, homesteads and other features of our primary industries. After all, I was a stock agent for thirty-four years.

After collating the book, I realised that the publication of even a small edition would need some support. I am indebted to the management of Elders Pastoral for their ready acceptance in acting as sponsor.

This book is sincerely dedicated to the farmers, graziers and stock agents who offered me unfailing friendship and warm hospitality for so many years.

Bruce Swann

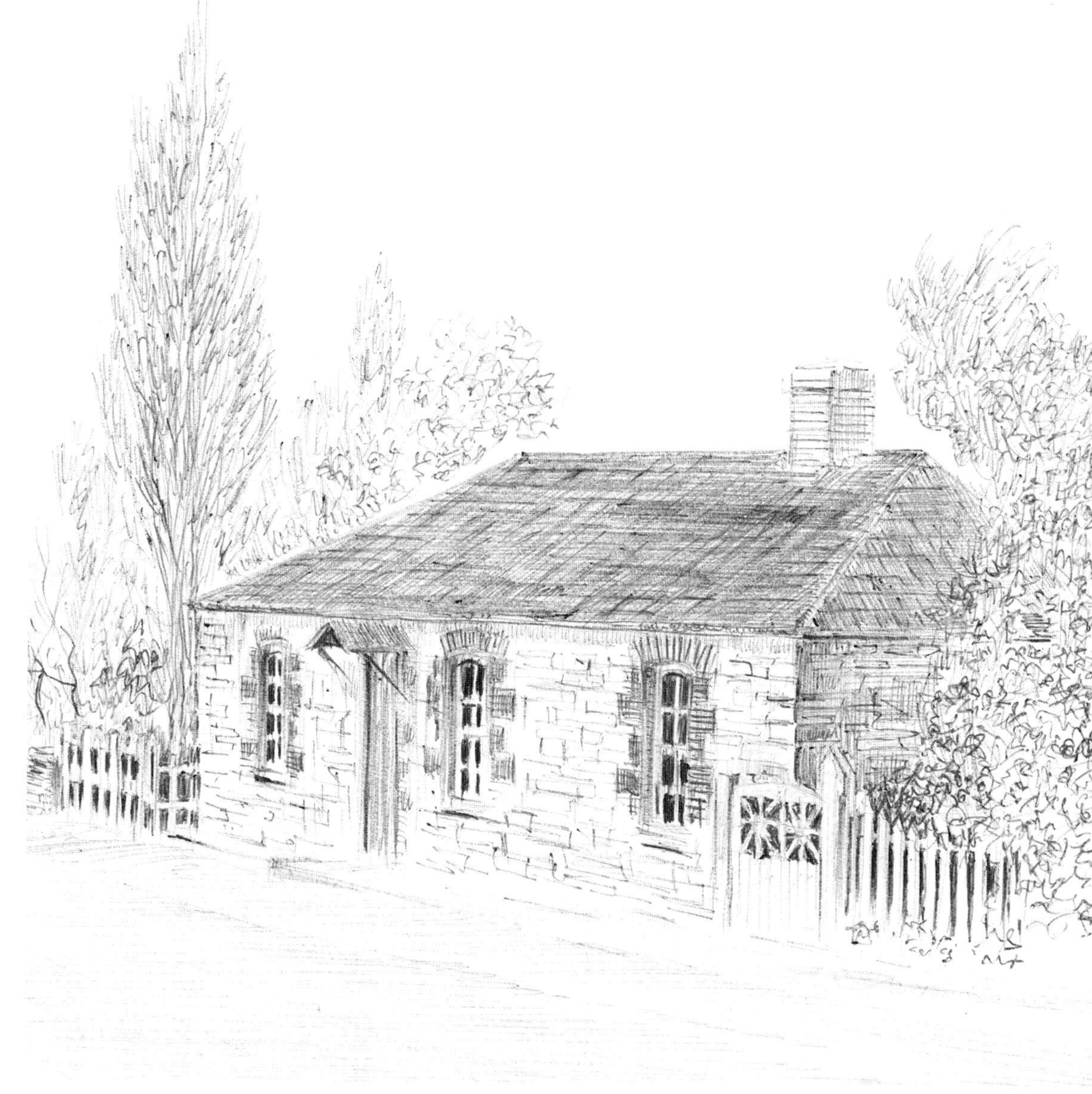

Dowie House, Willunga
A slate-roofed cottage built in about 1850.

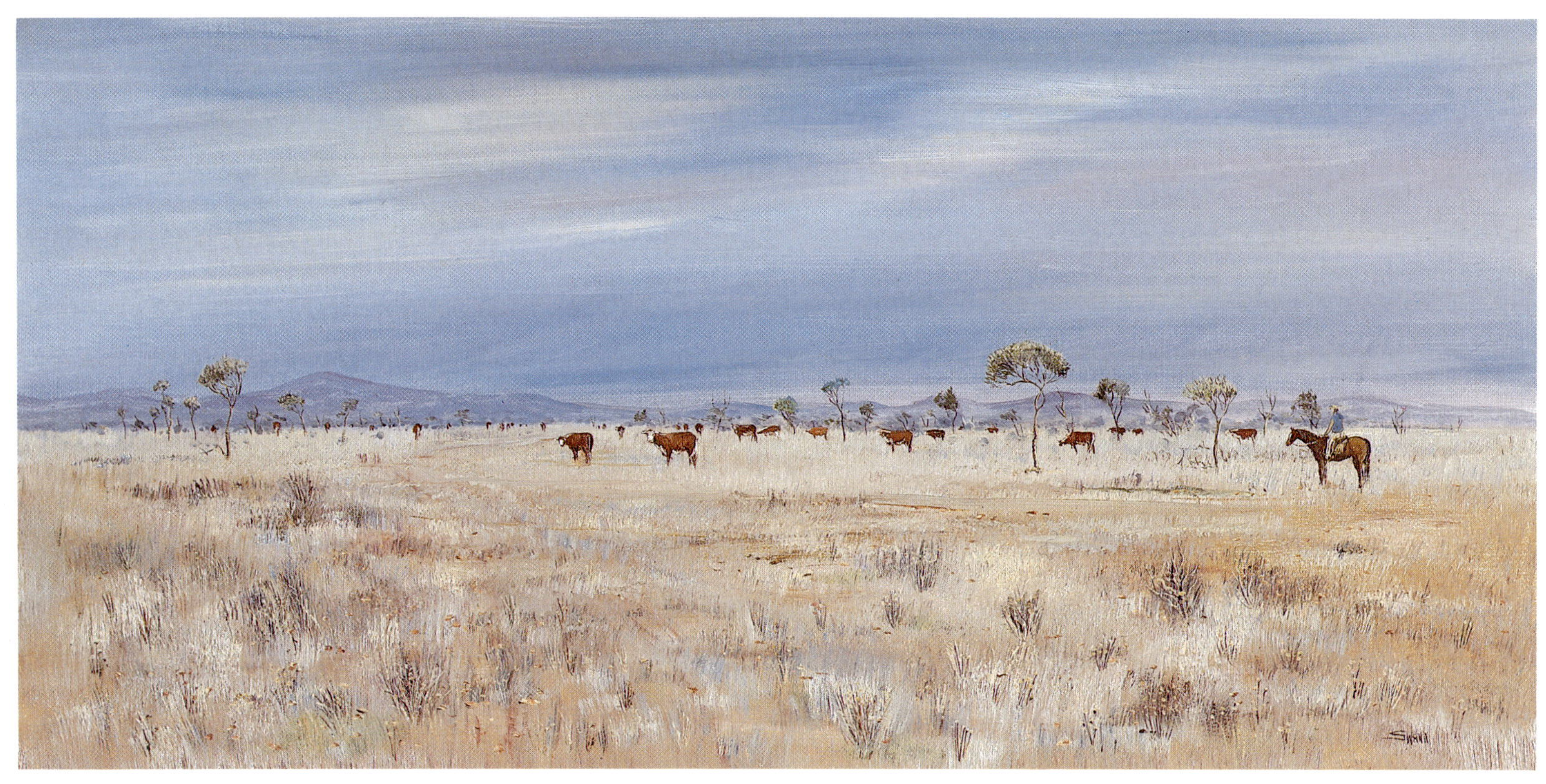

Cattle on Todmorden Station,
Oodnadatta

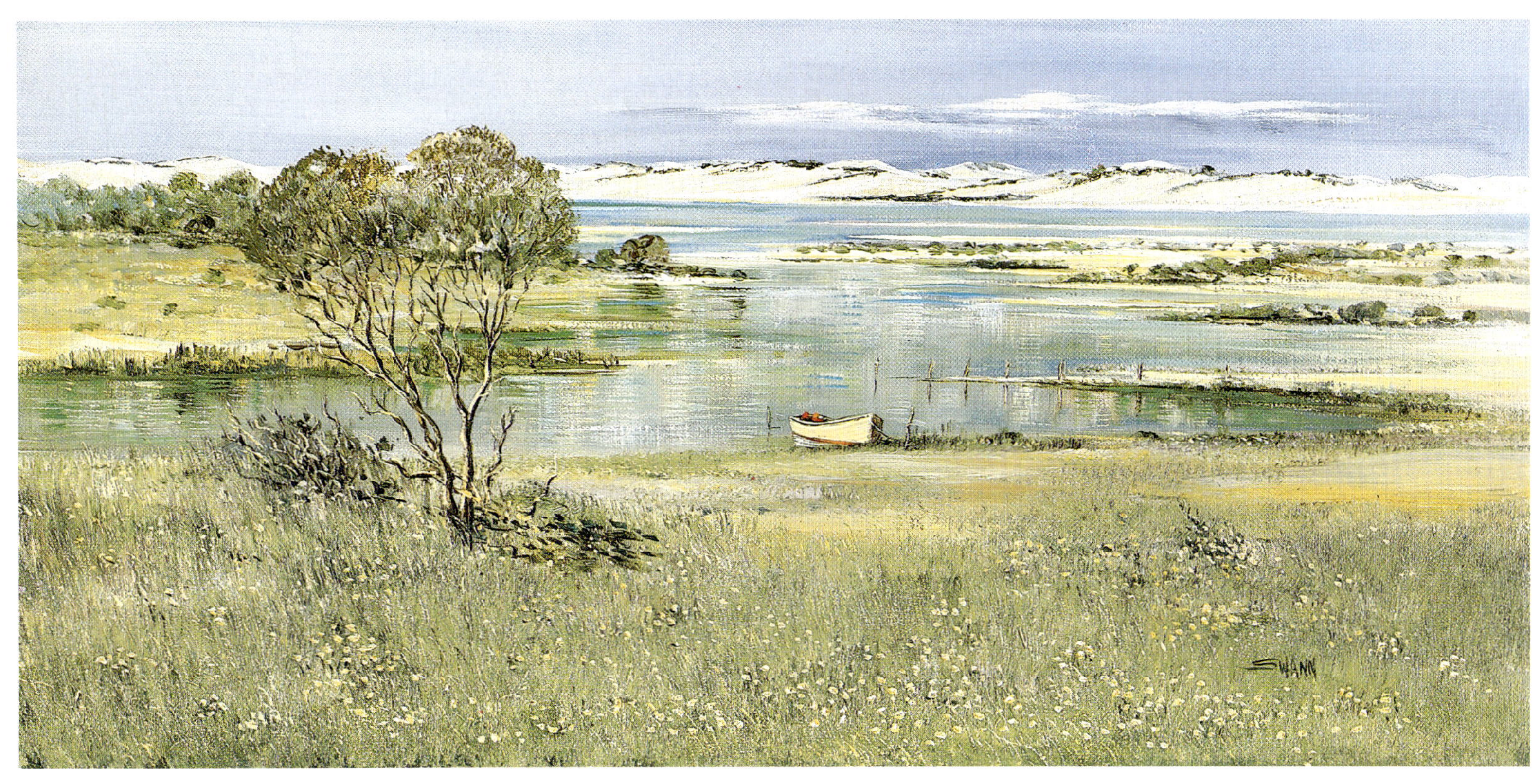

The Coorong at Salt Creek

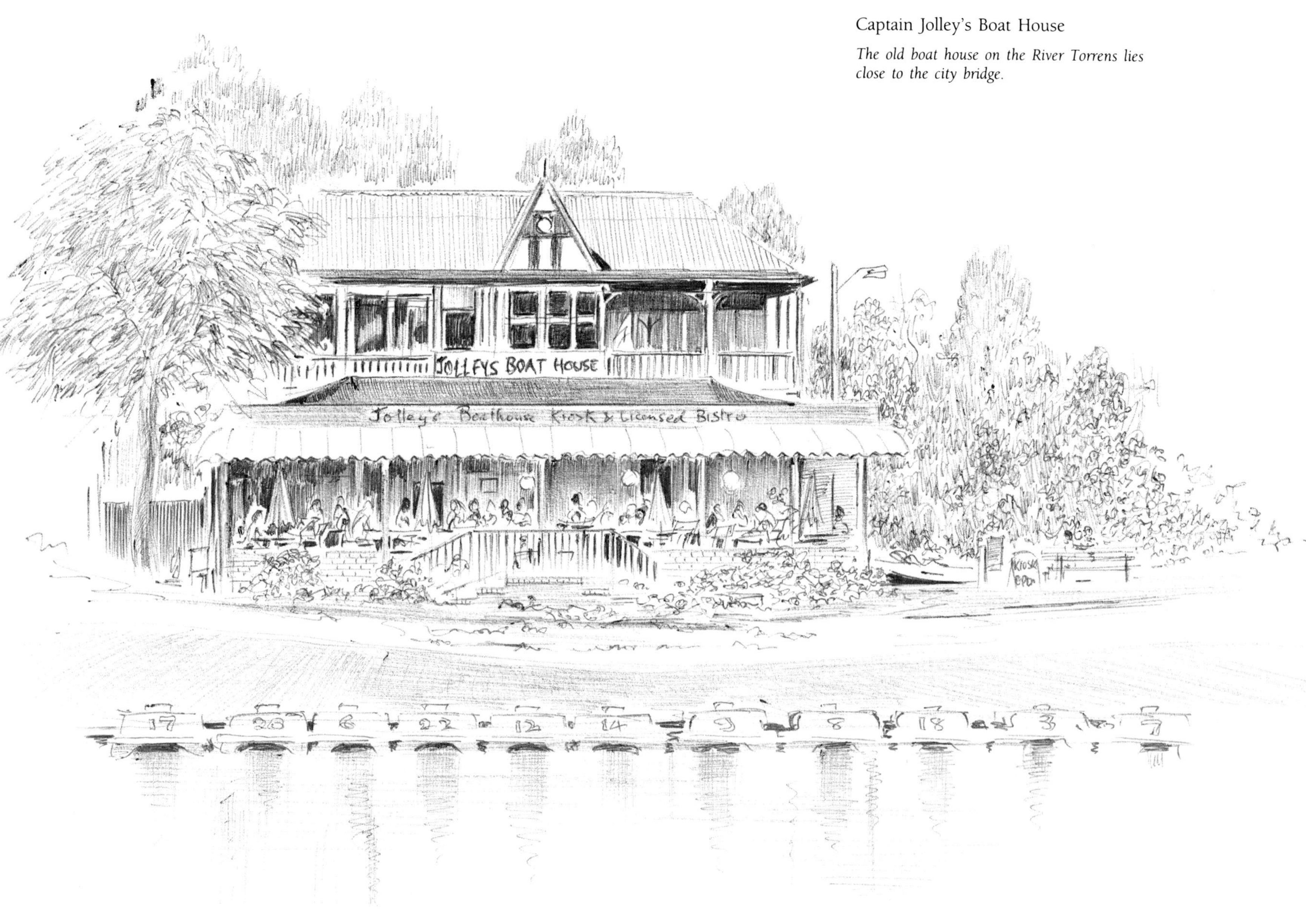

Captain Jolley's Boat House

The old boat house on the River Torrens lies close to the city bridge.

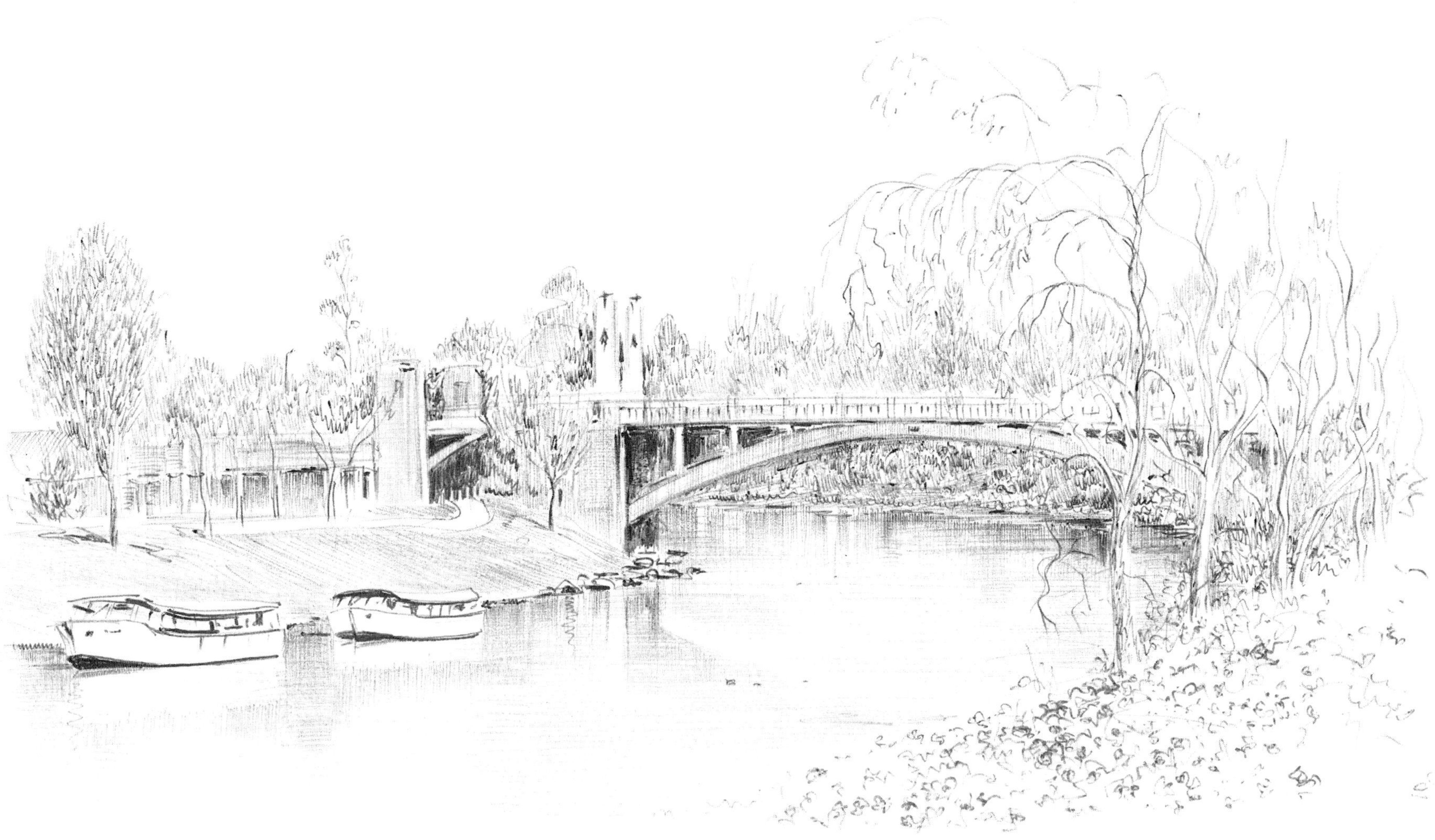

The city bridge with Popeye I and
Popeye II in the foreground

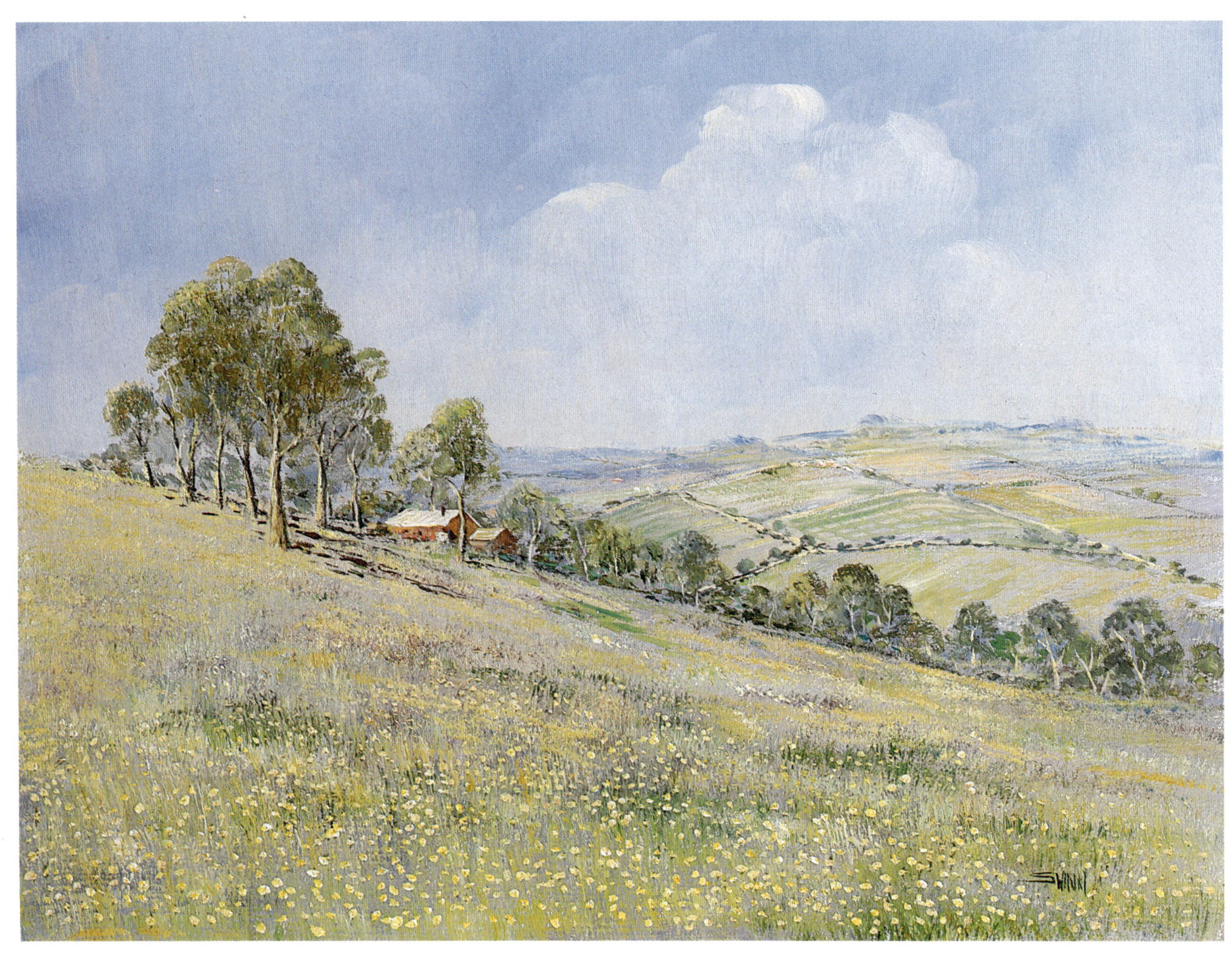

In the Mount Lofty Ranges

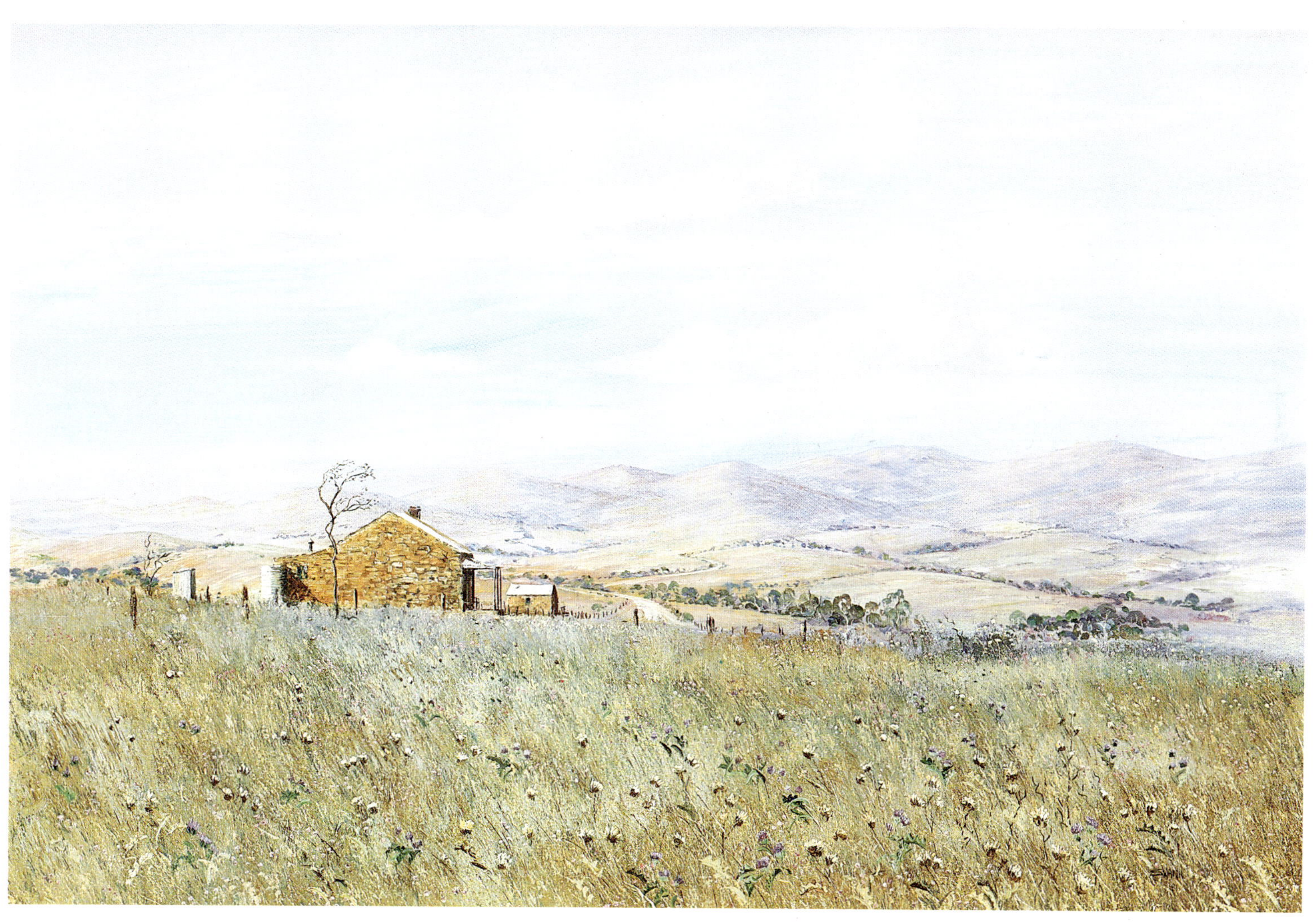

Settler's farmstead in the Flinders
Ranges

The Russian Orthodox Church of
St Nicholas, Wayville

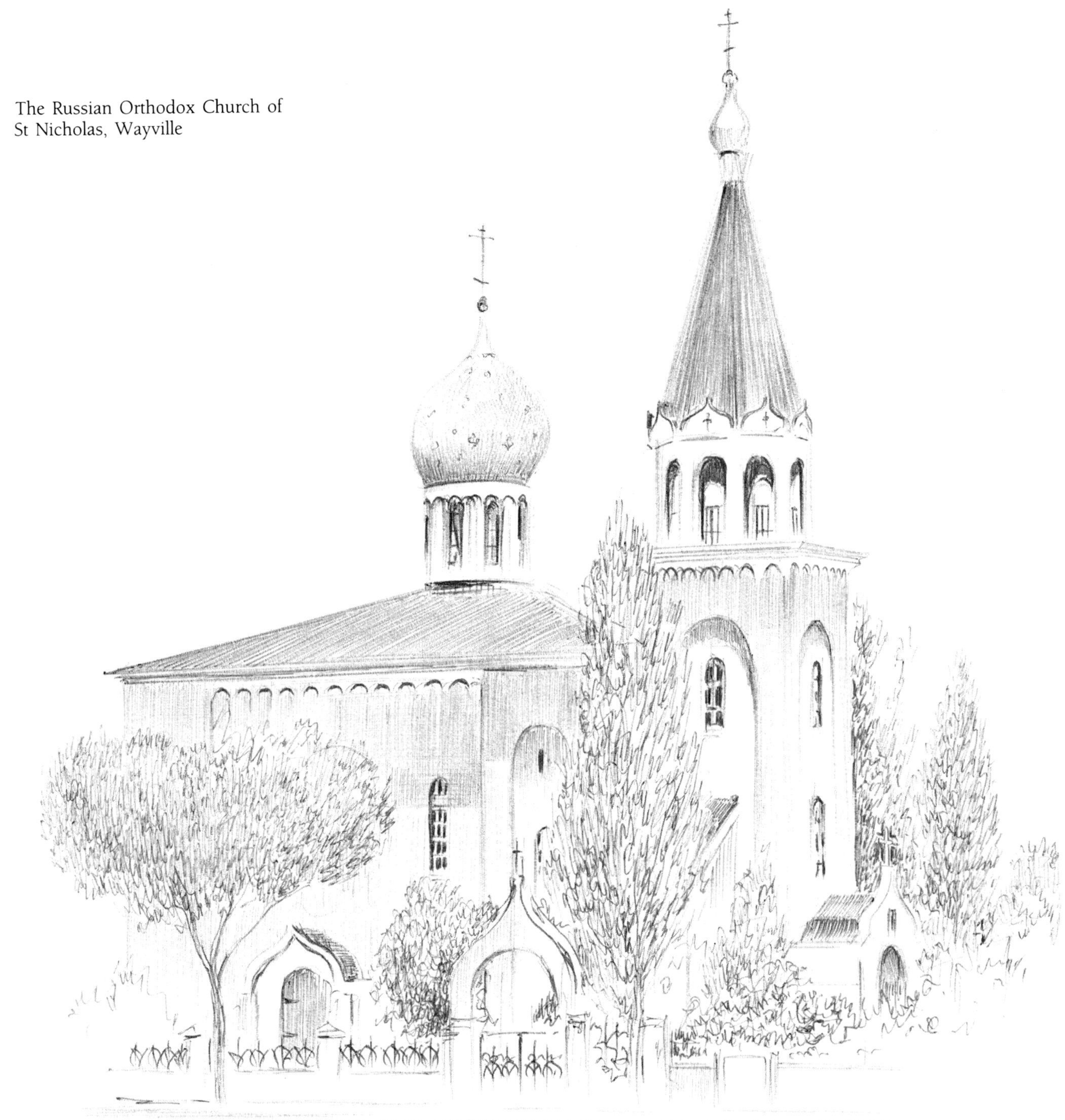

Beehive Corner, Rundle Mall, Adelaide

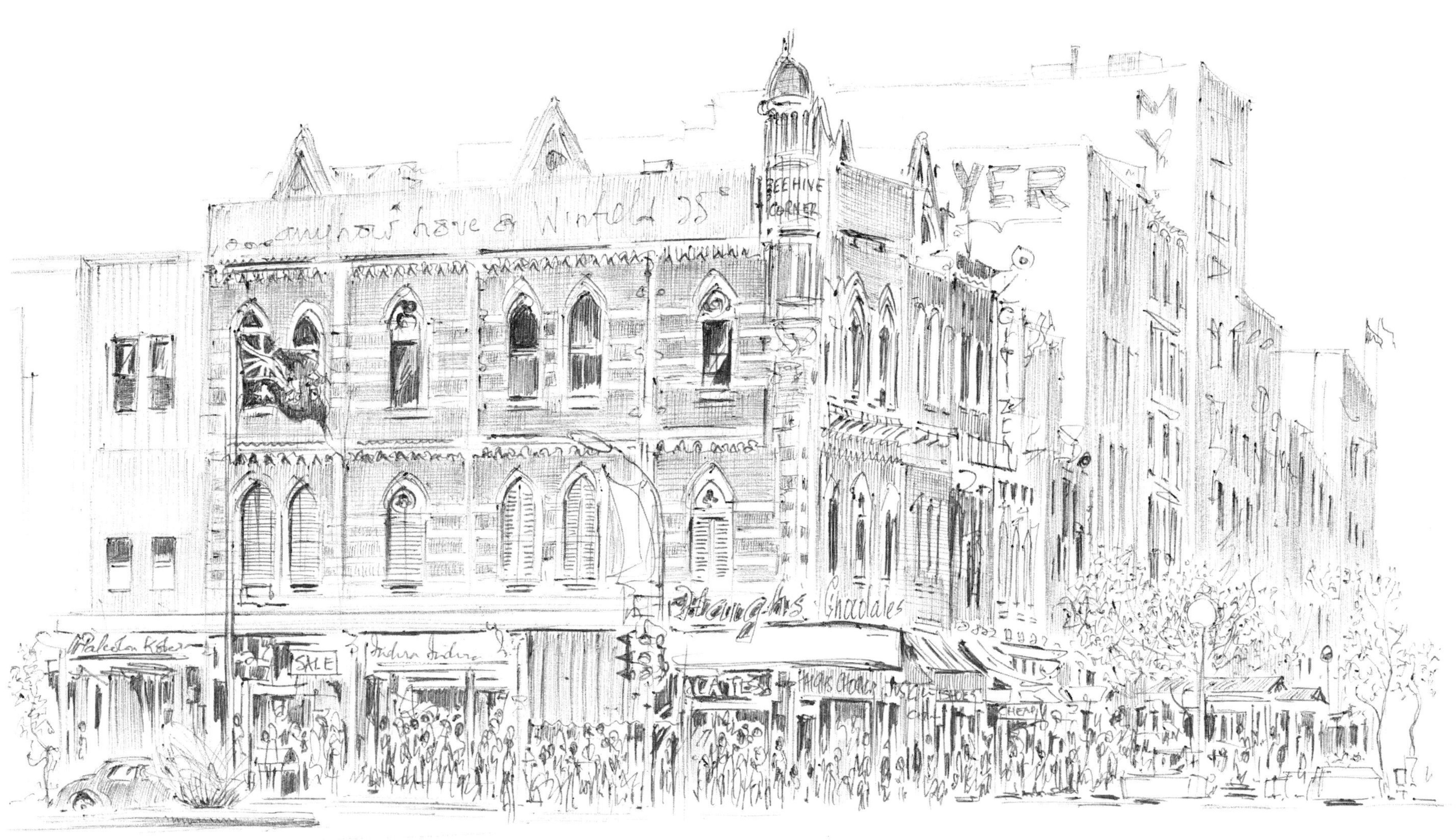

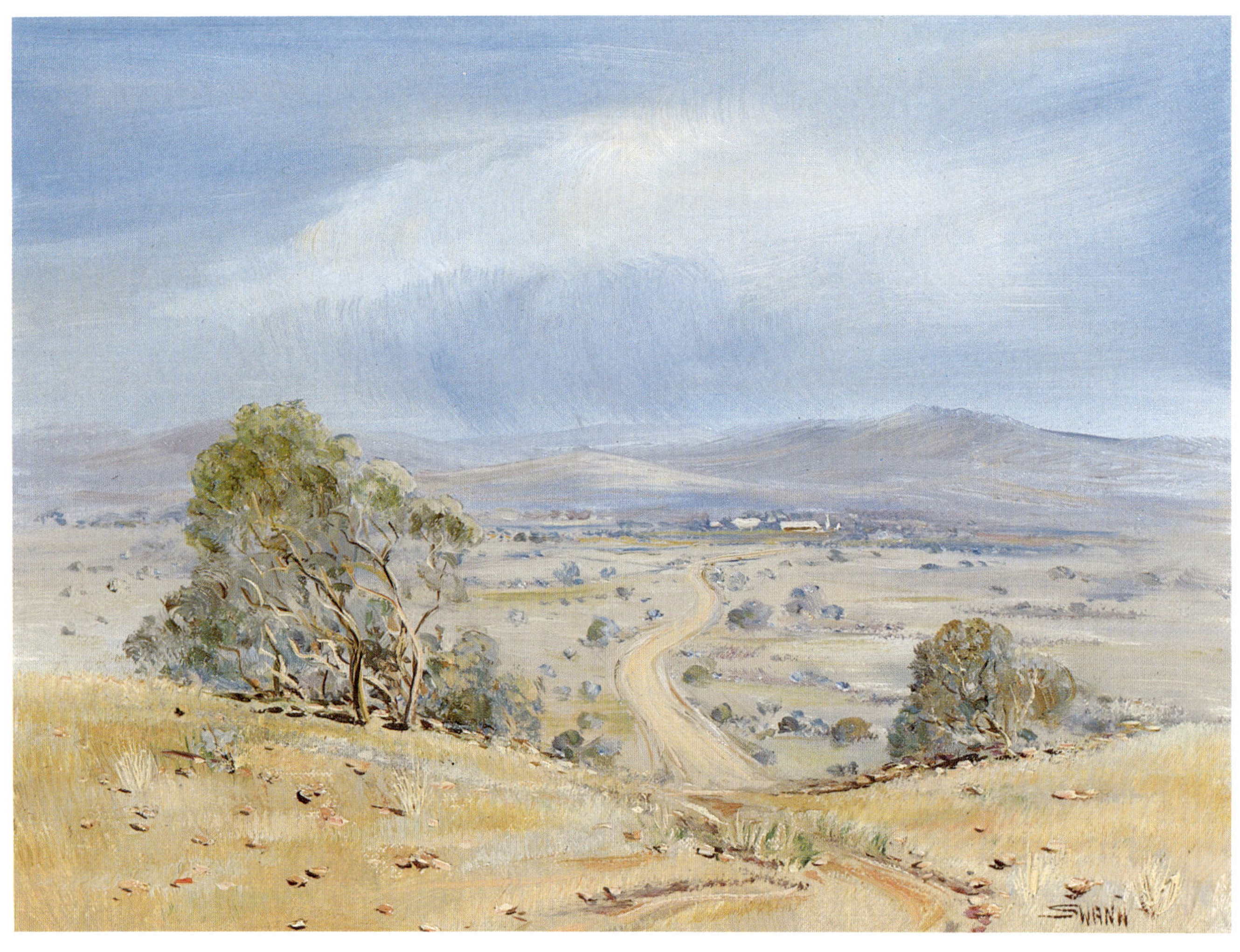

The track, lower Flinders Ranges

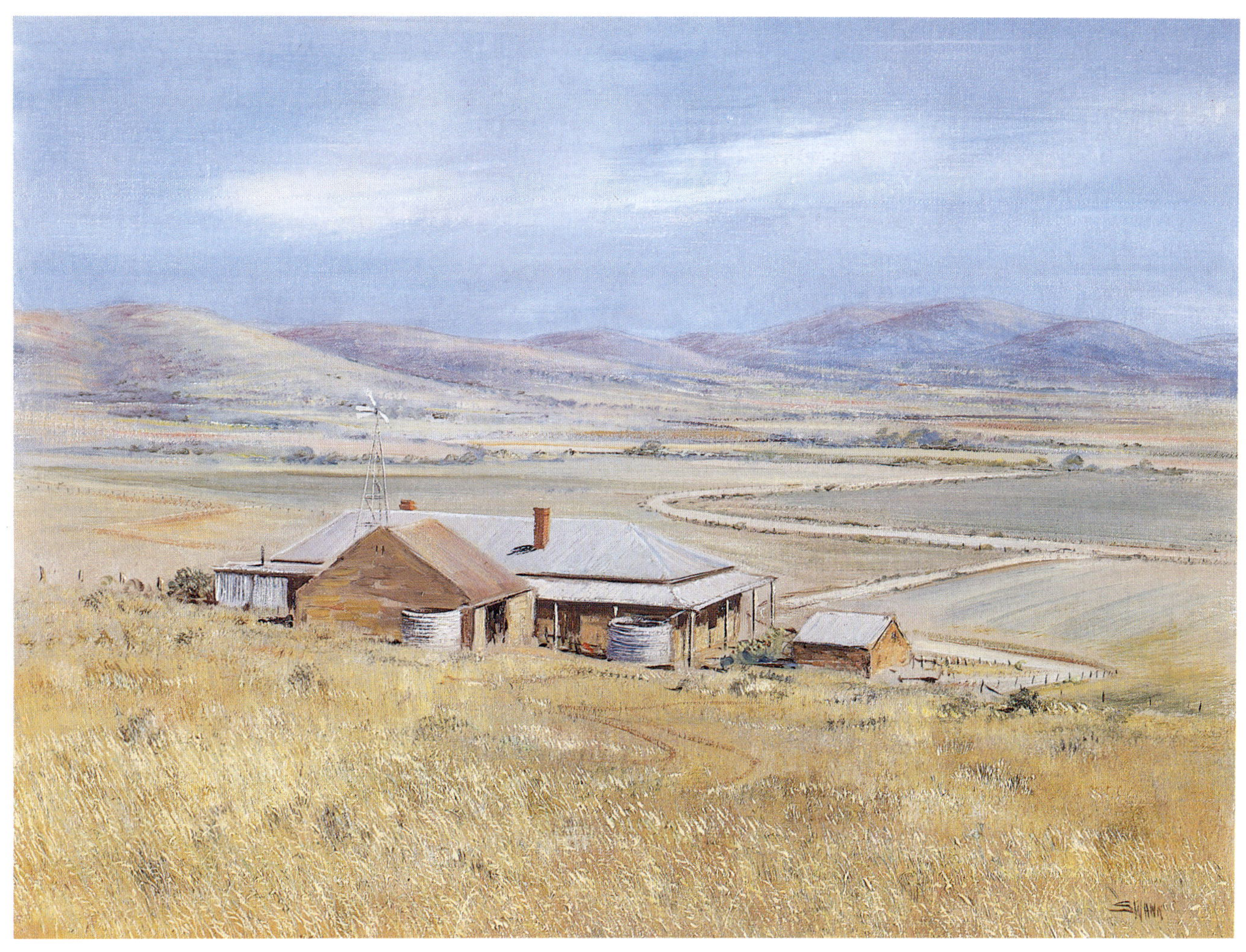

Northern pastures

*Sitting and drawing this farmhouse brought
back fond memories of a big, old kitchen with
a flagstone floor, and a roast leg of lamb
framed by the wood oven door.*

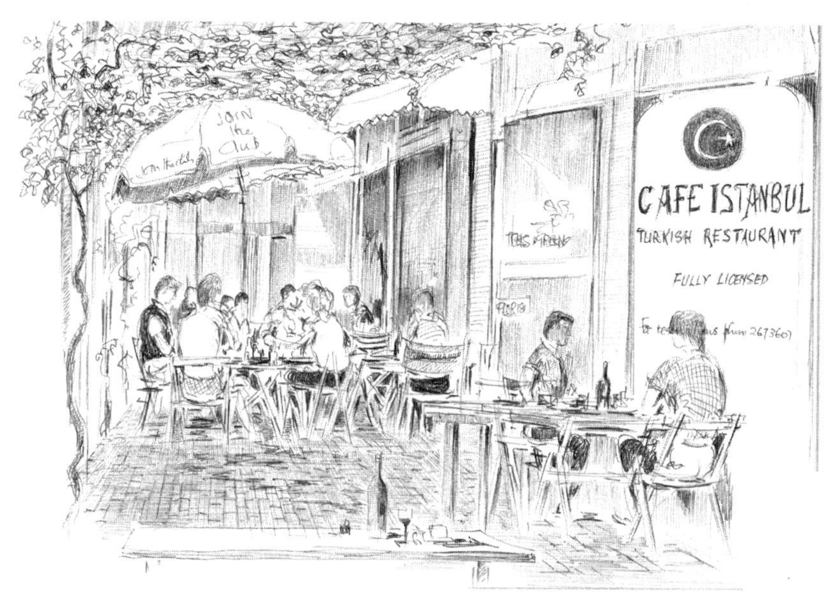

Sidewalk cafes and vine-covered
courtyards in North Adelaide's busy
Melbourne Street

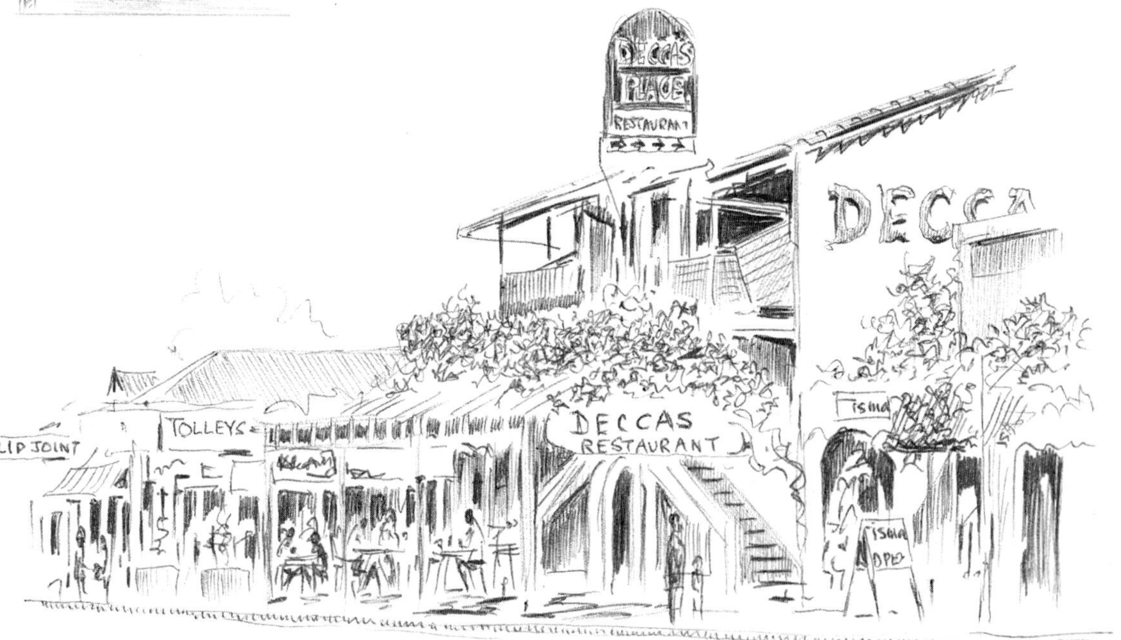

Elder gallery, Melbourne Street

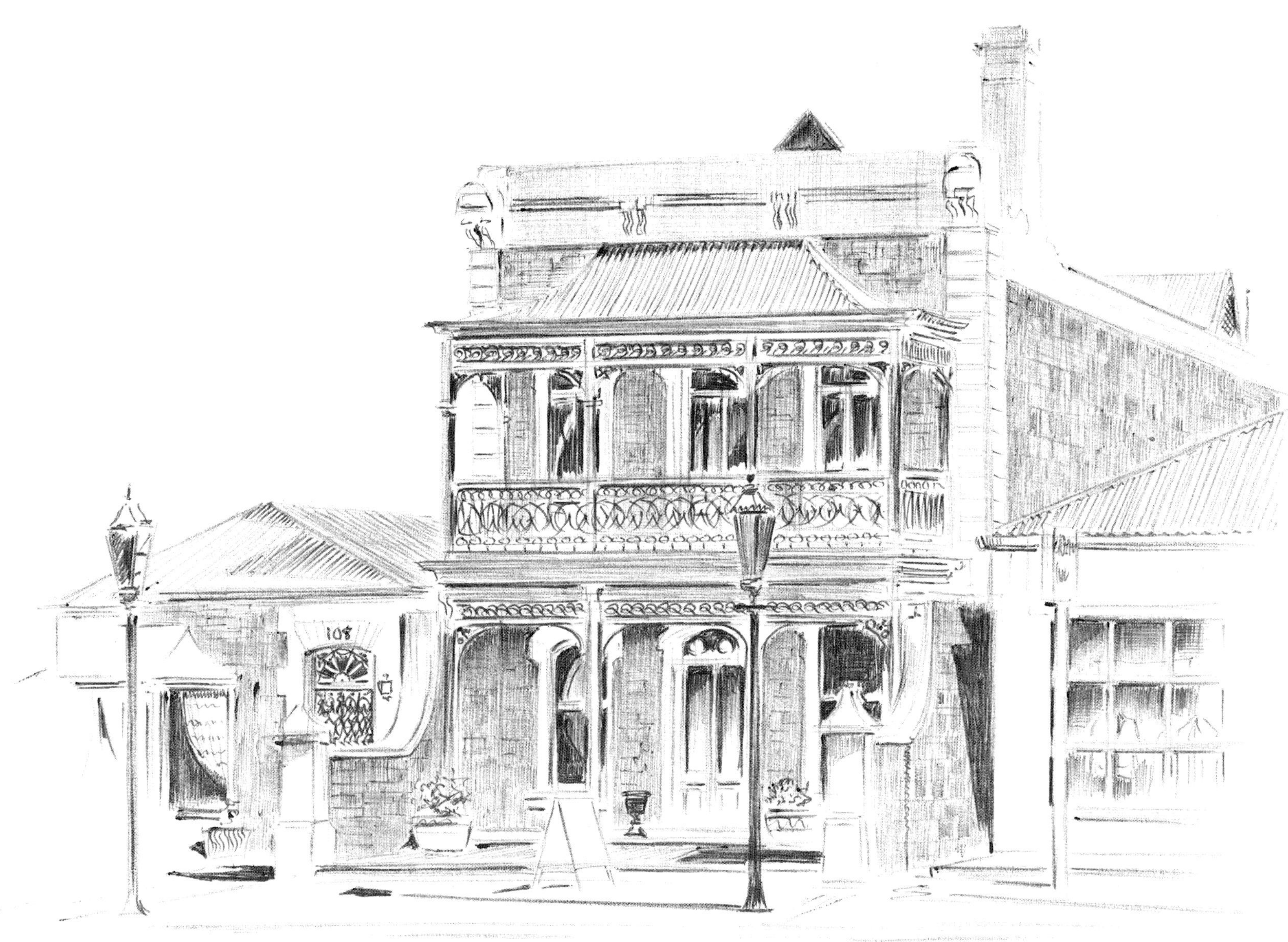

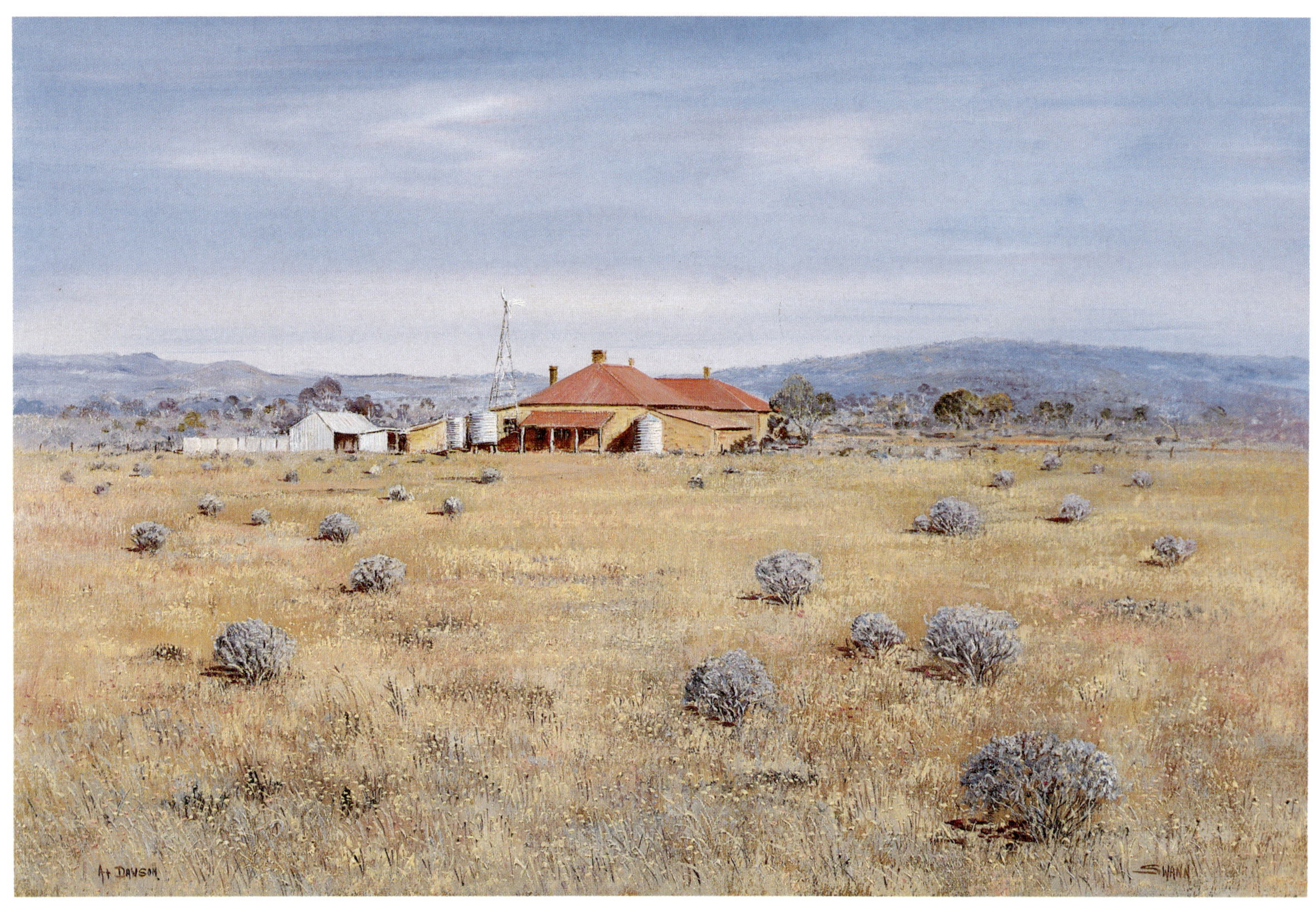

On the outskirts of Dawson township
in the north of the State

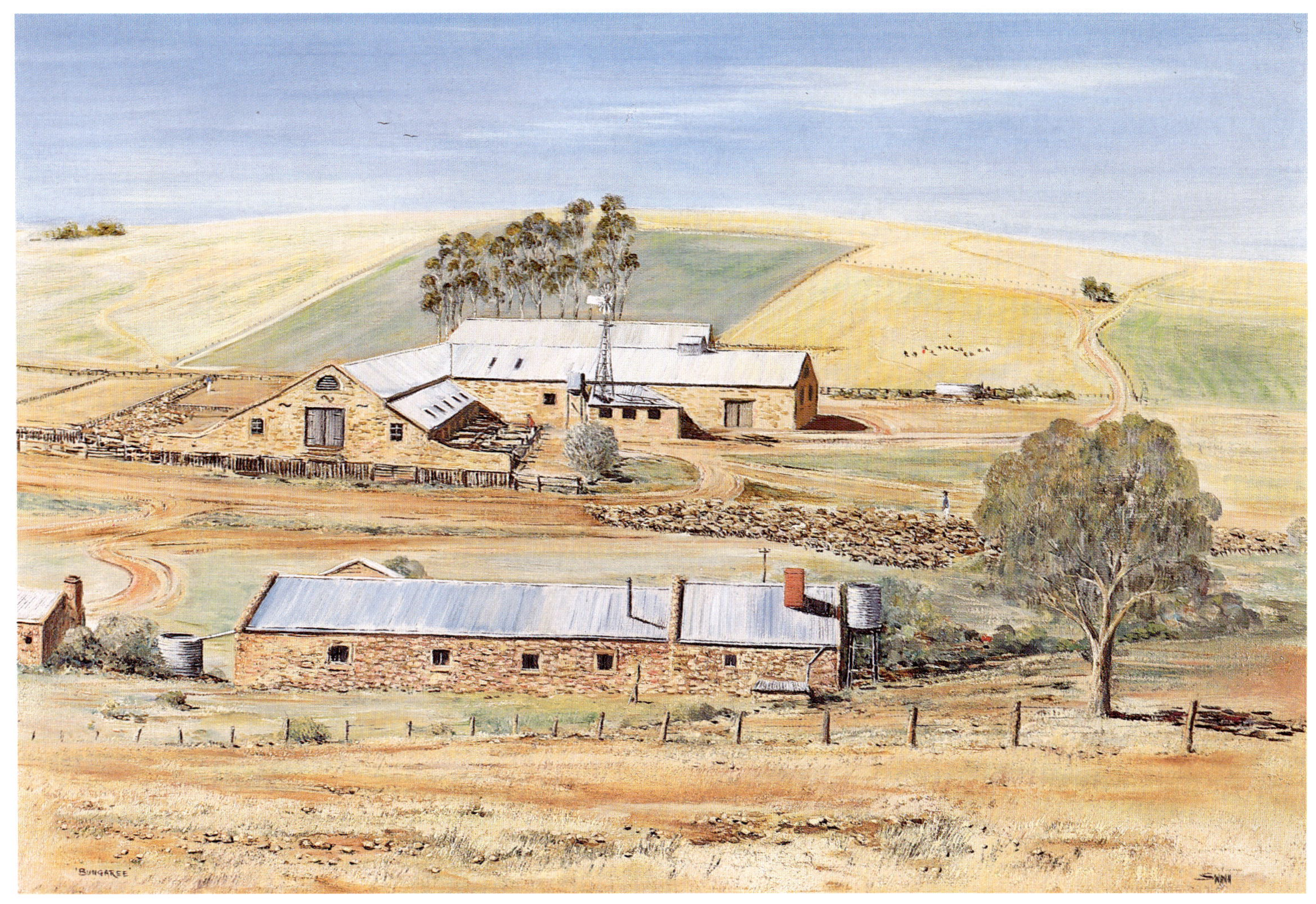

Bungaree woolshed, Clare

Bungaree Station, home of the historic merino stud, was founded in 1841. Before the advent of machine shearing the wool clip was shorn by forty-four blade shearers. A total of 200 men were employed for the shearing season.

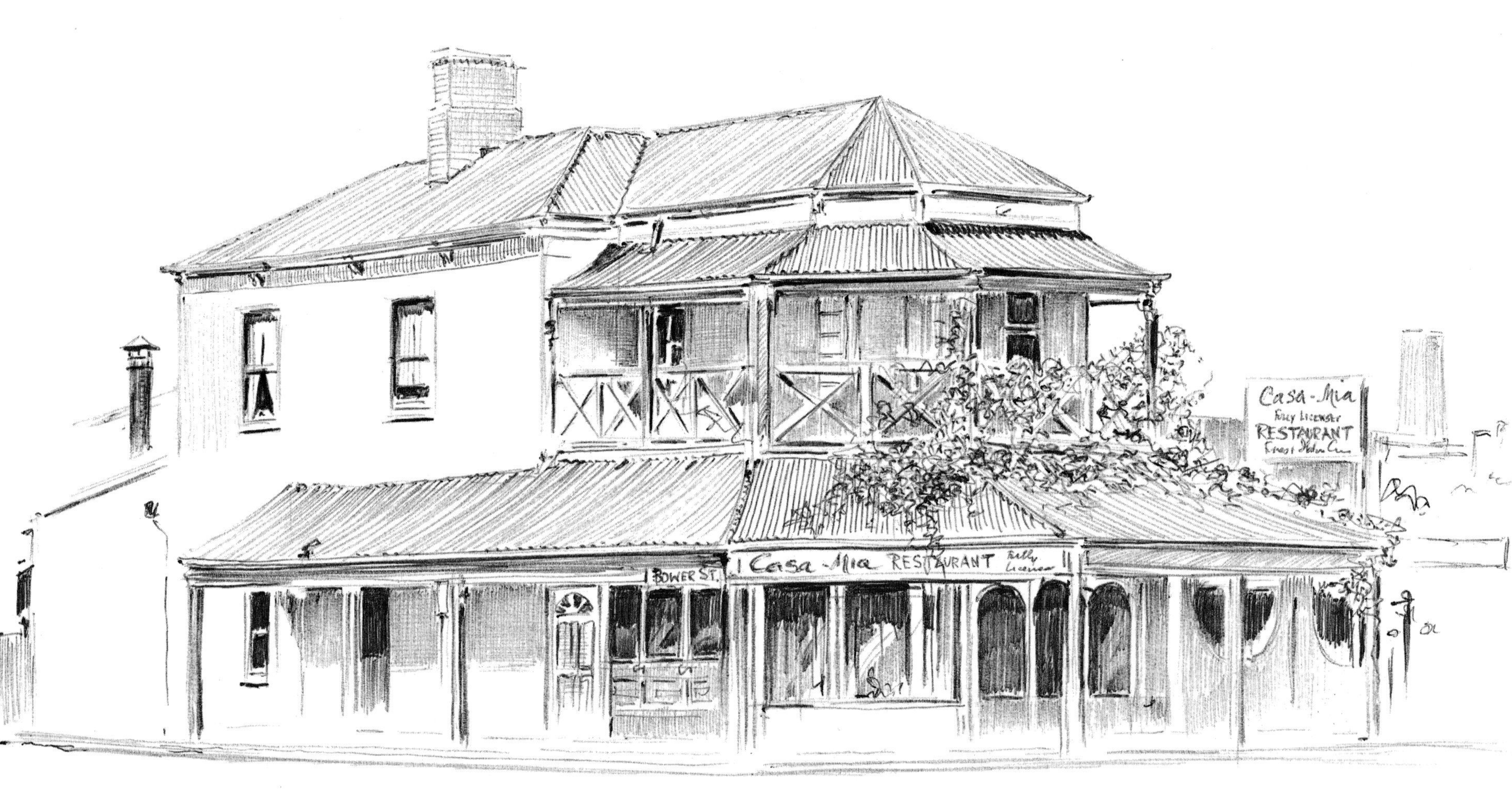

Casa Mia, Melbourne Street

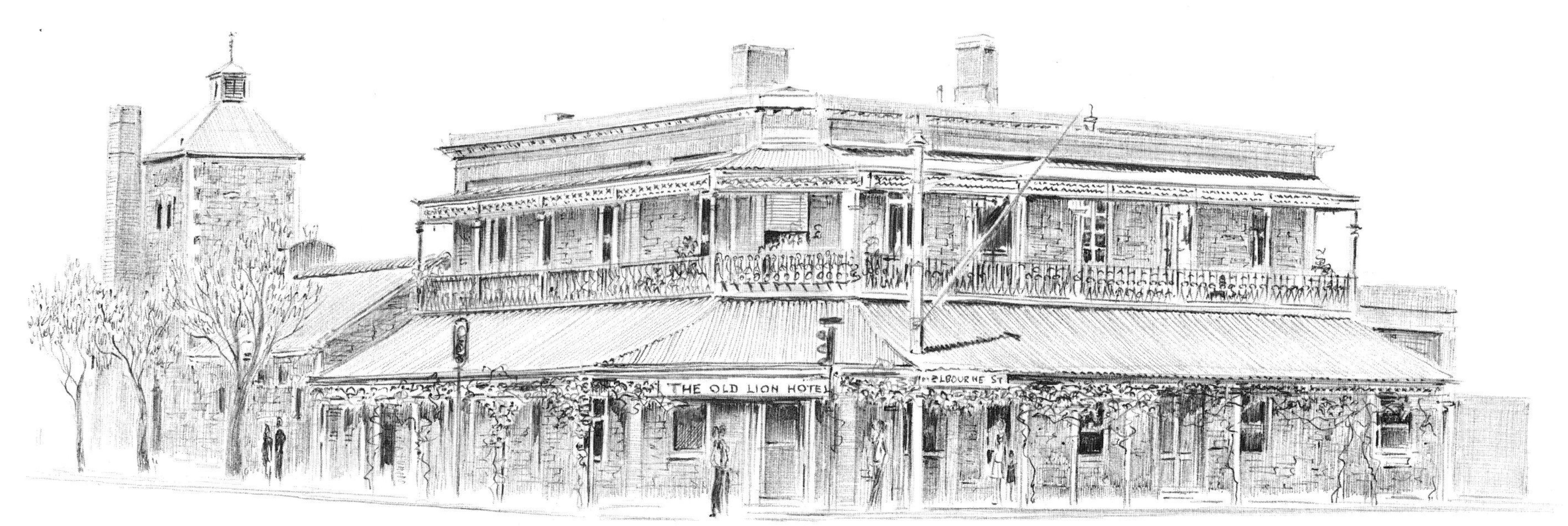

The Old Lion Hotel, Melbourne Street

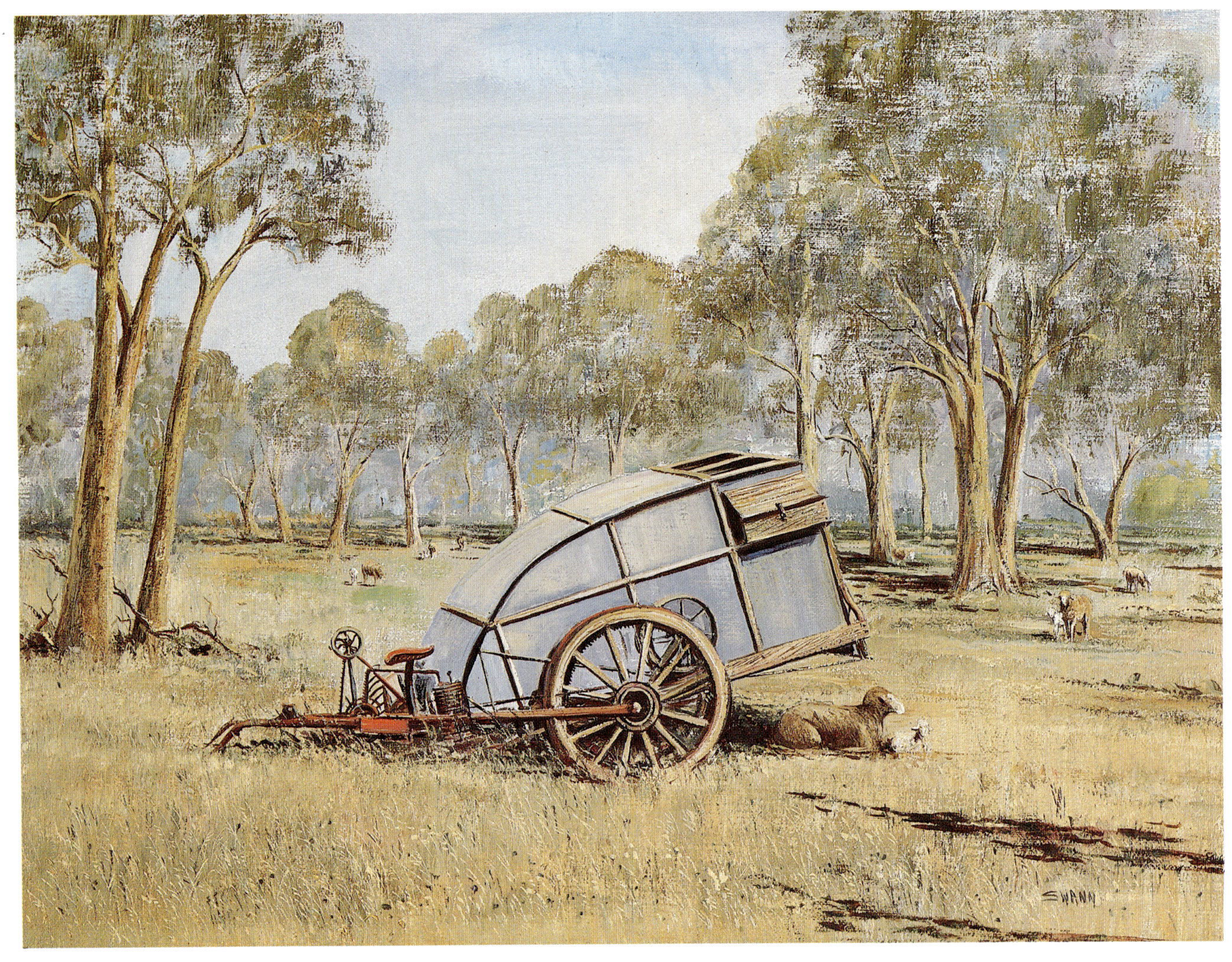

Old stripper complete with wooden
tool box, River Murray flats

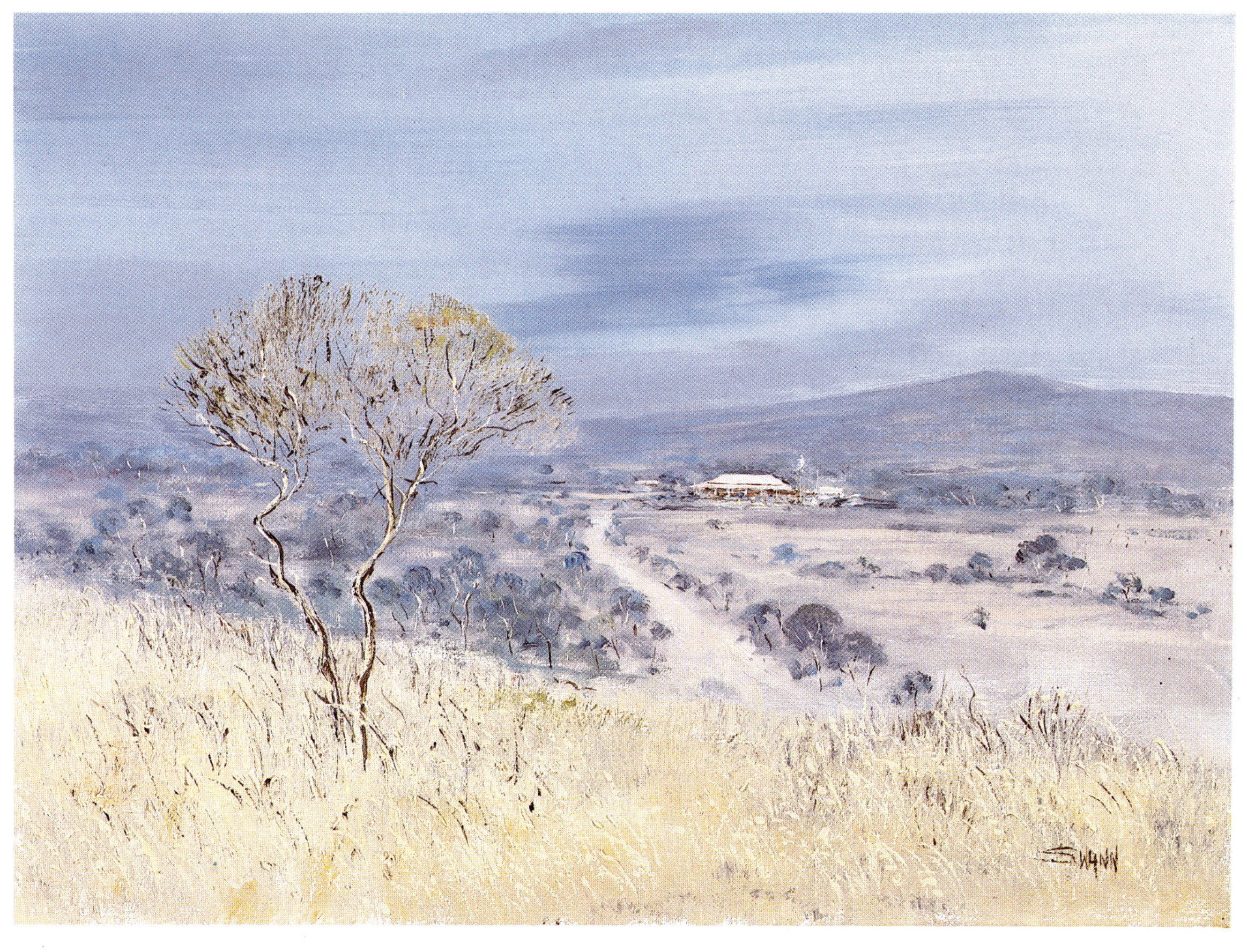

Northern nocturn

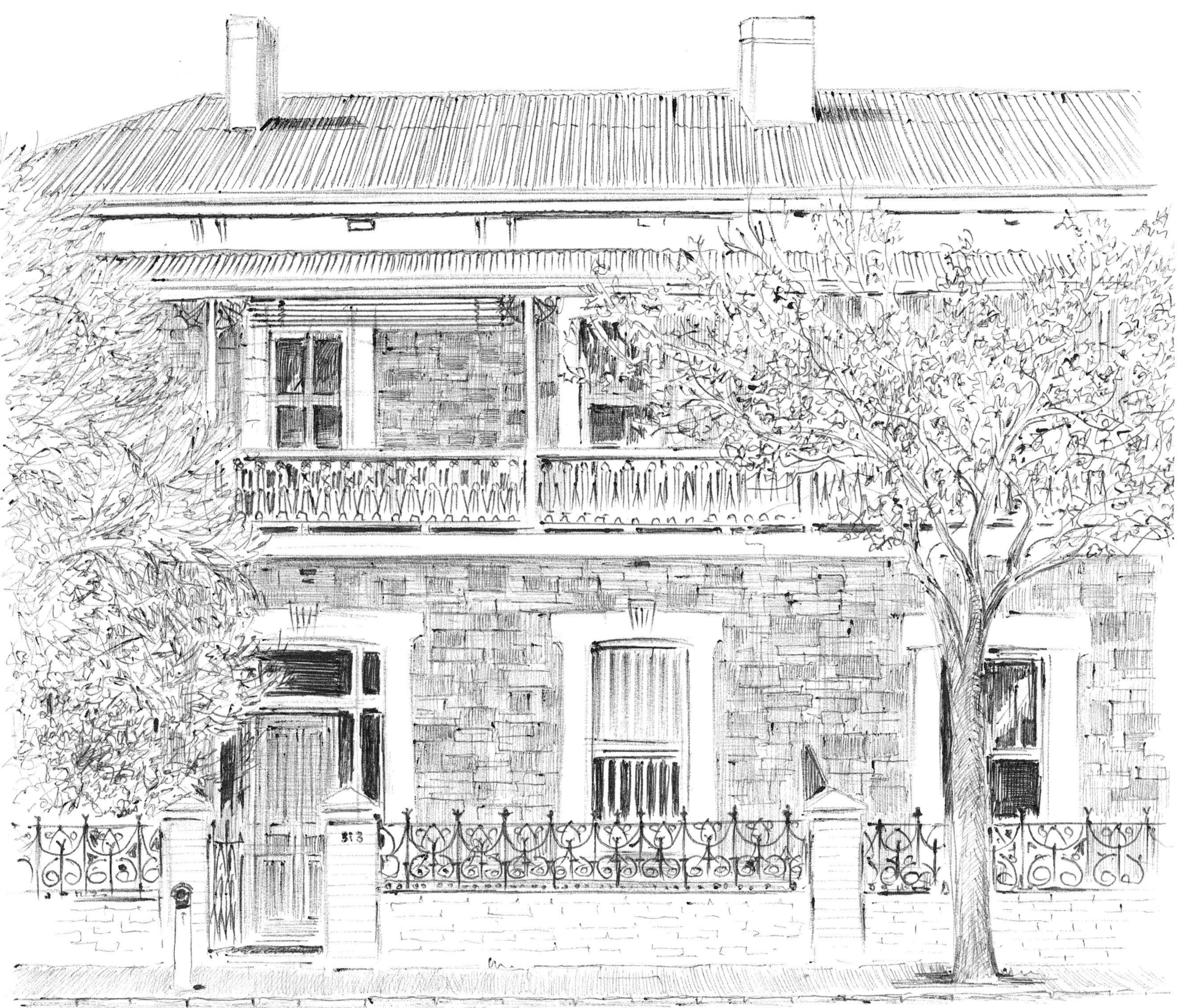

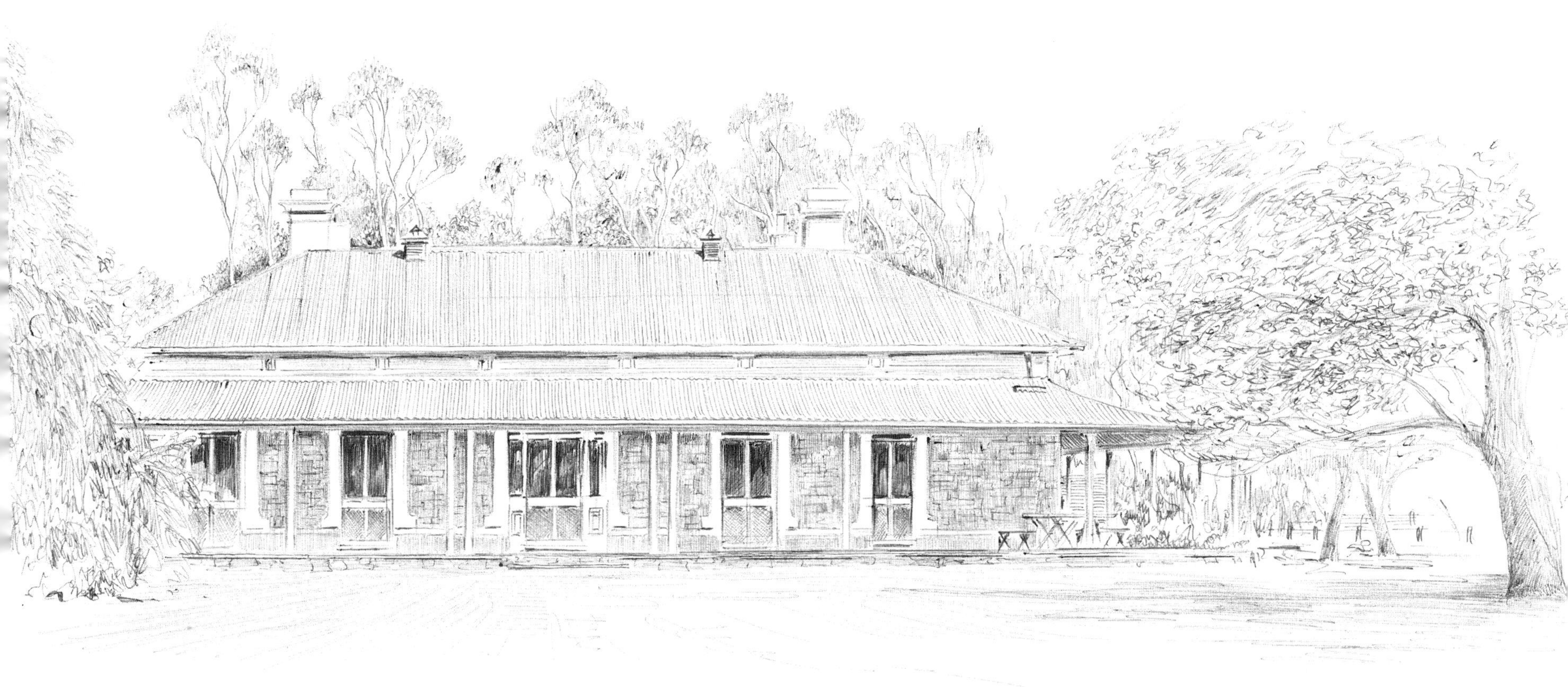

The Levels, Pooraka

This elegant colonial homestead is now part of the Elders pastoral livestock holding area.

313 Gilles Street, Adelaide

A terrace house built about 1860 in the south-east corner of the city.

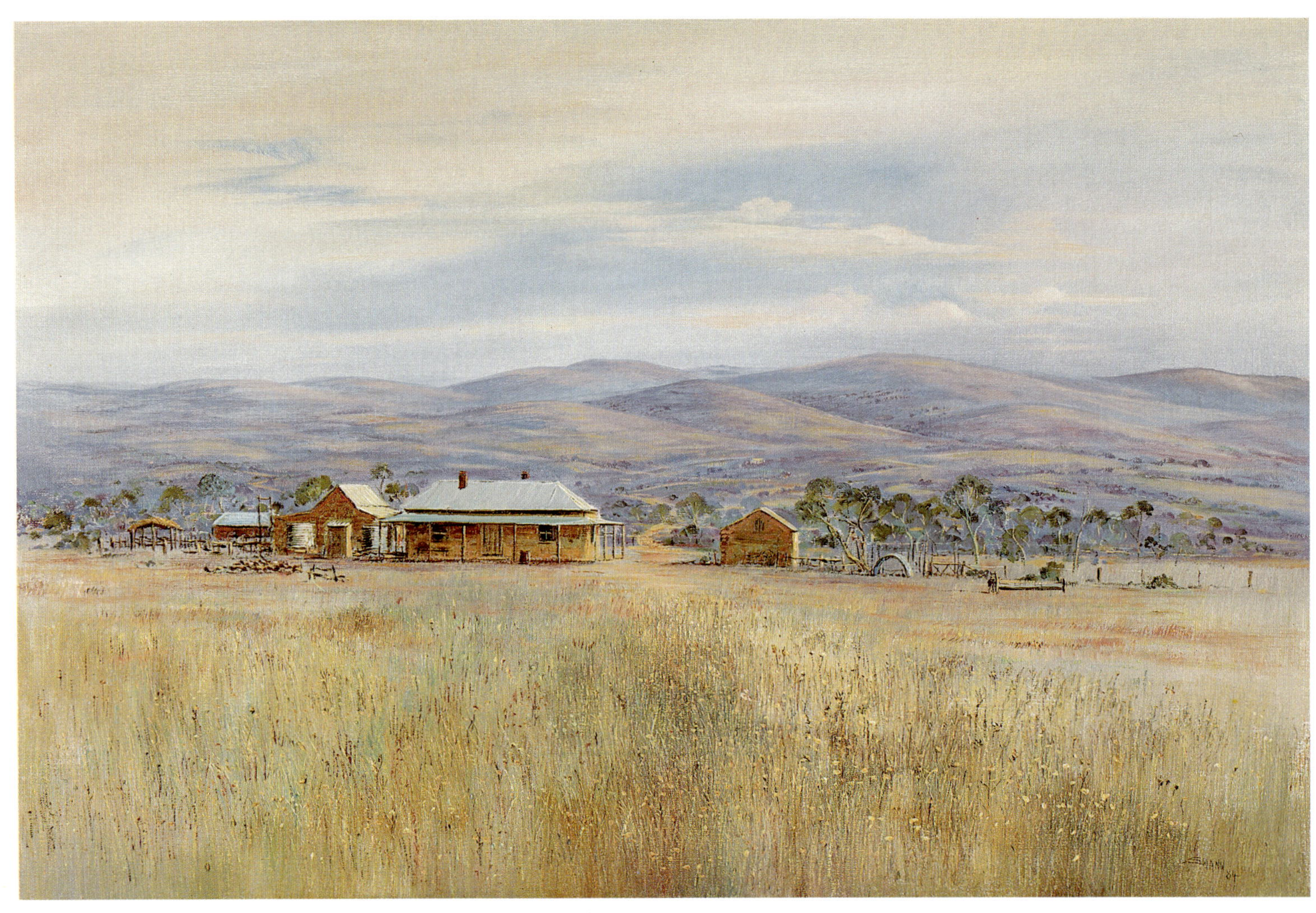

Evening in the Flinders Ranges

In the summers of the north it is wise to sketch and paint in the early morning or late afternoon. The sometimes harsh landscape then softens to a gentler beauty.

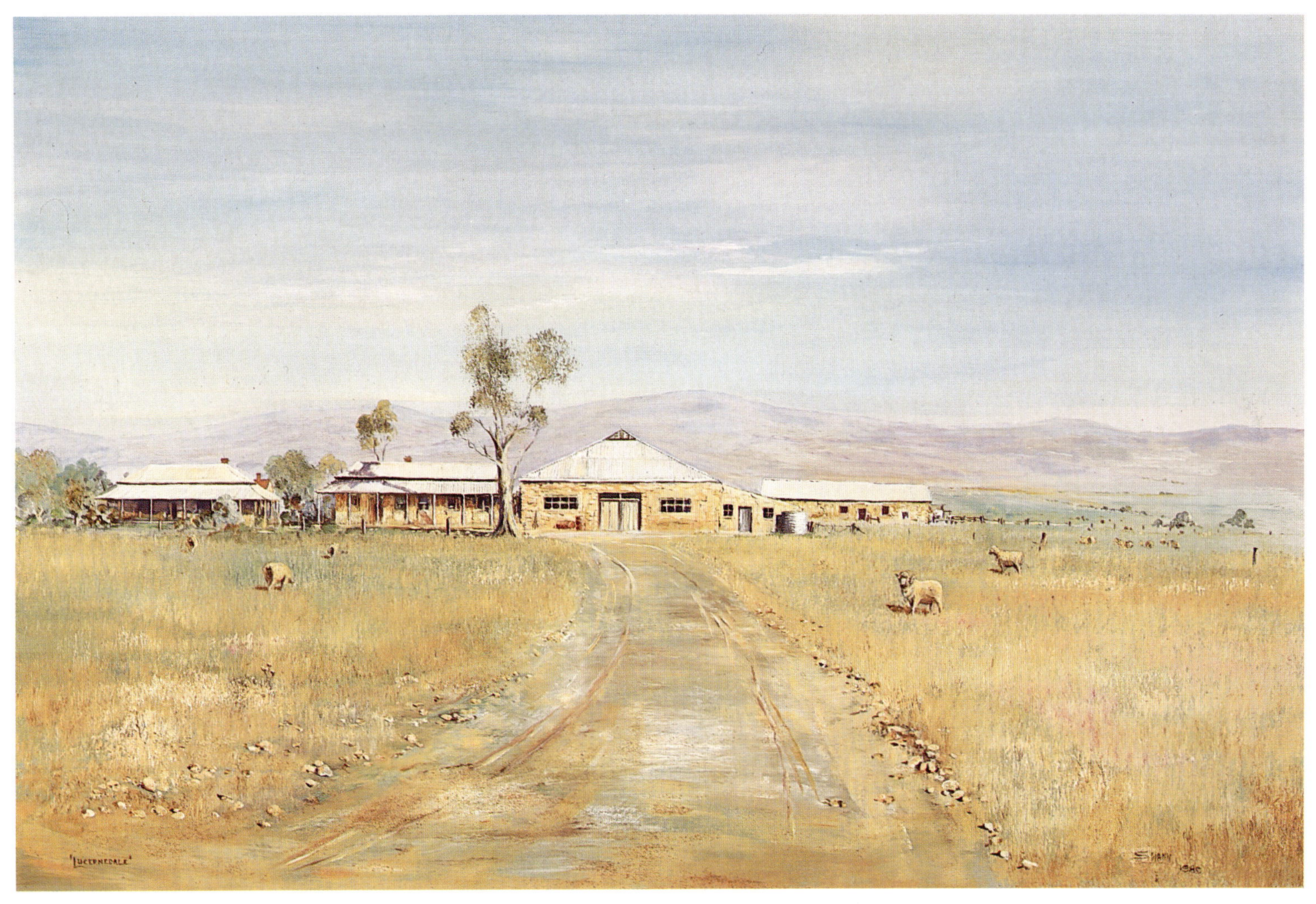

Lucernedale homestead, Mount Bryan

The Lucernedale merino sheep stud was founded in 1884 by Henry Collins. This hardy settler started life as a bullocky in Burra and lived to the age of ninety-seven.

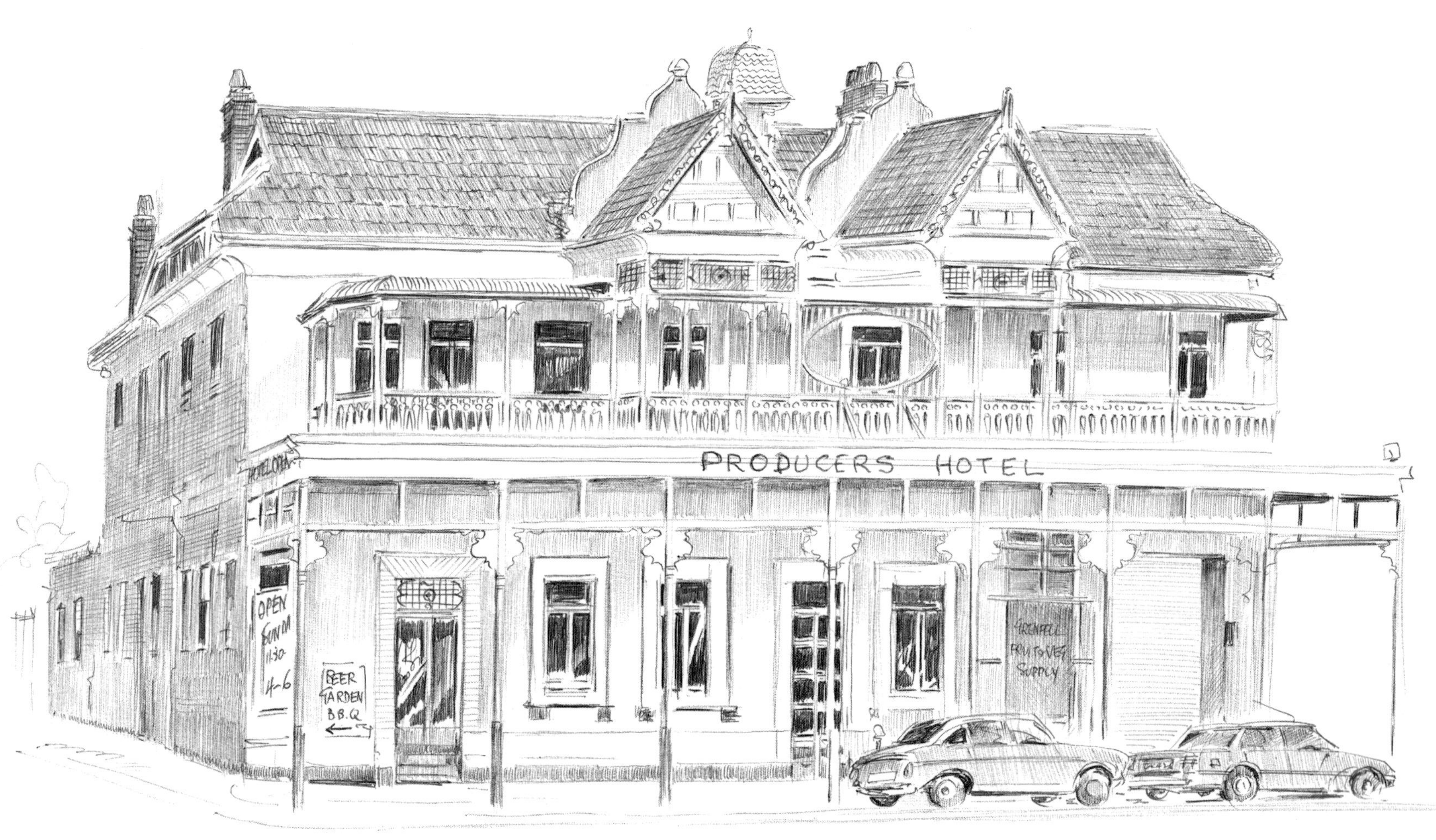

The Producers Hotel, Grenfell Street,
opposite the east end fruit and
vegetable market

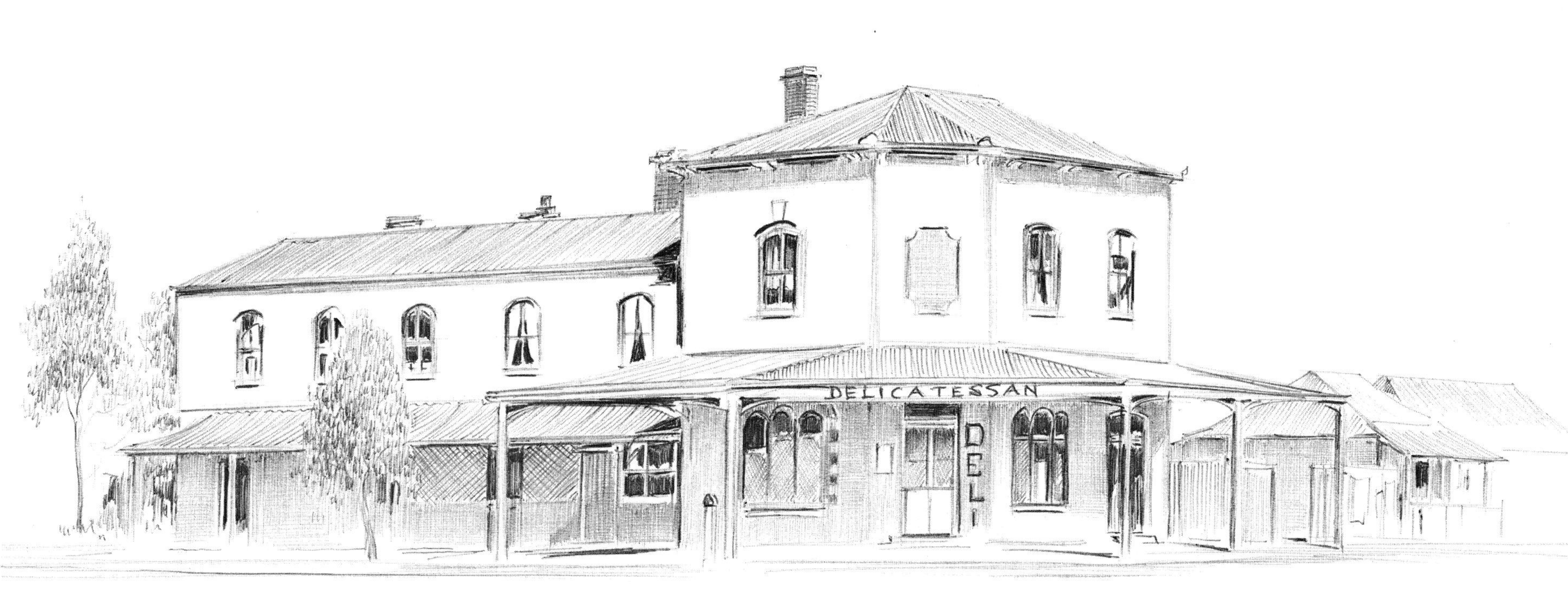

Corner deli, Finniss Street, North
Adelaide

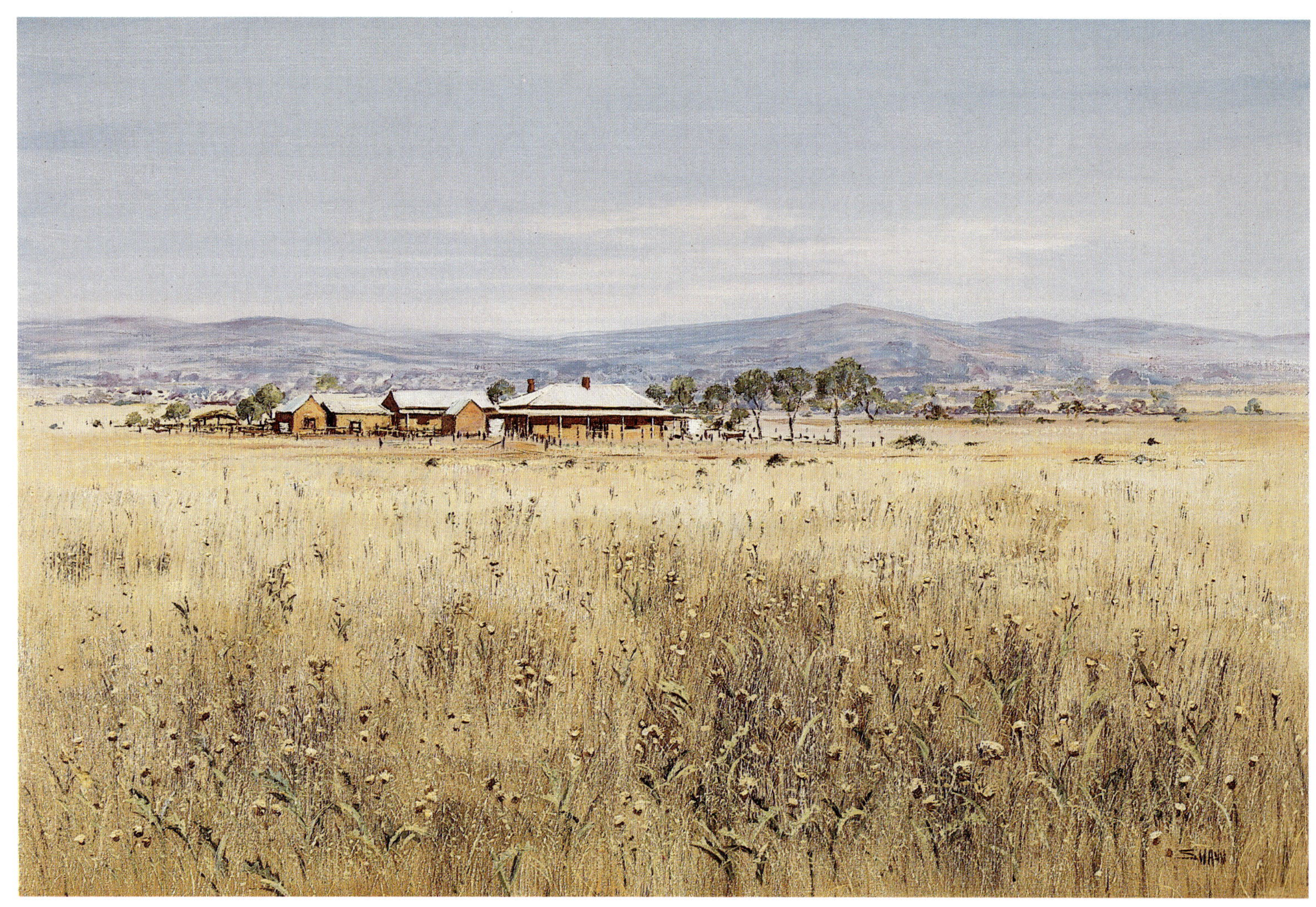

Summer thistles

As young plants these are sometimes used as stockfeed while the dry flowers make attractive decorations. But they need careful handling—the thorns are needle sharp.

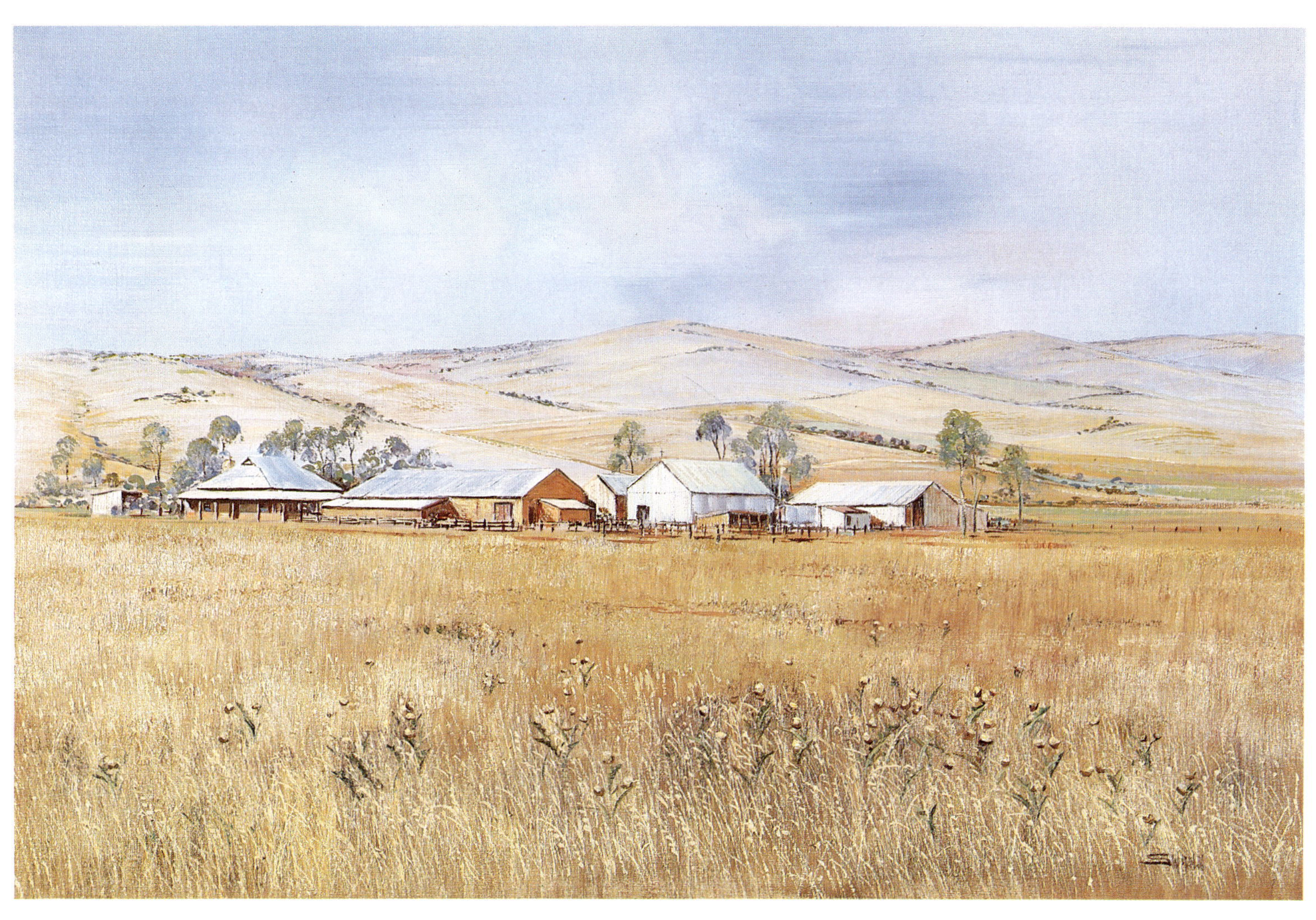

Kybunga Farm in the grain-growing
Mid North

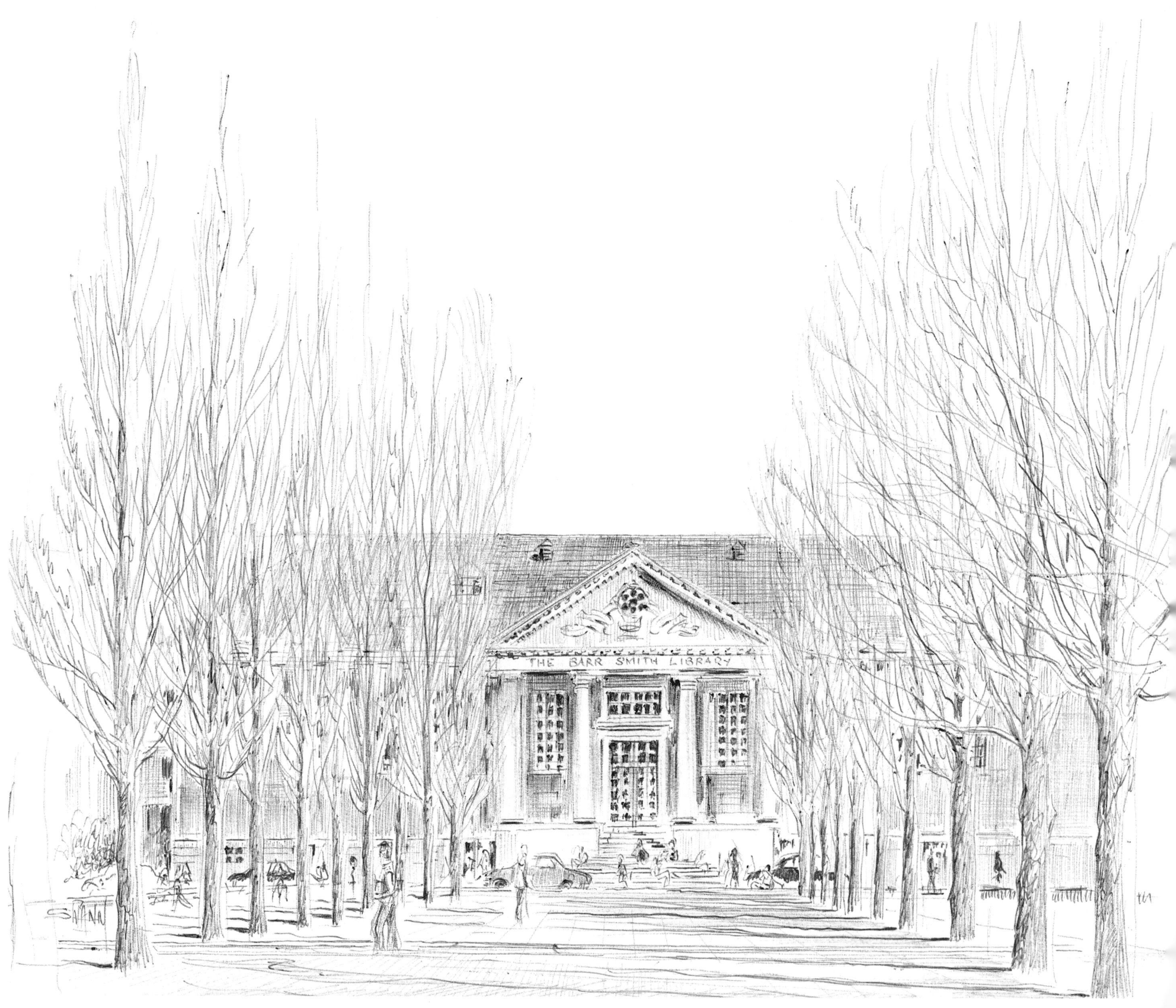

THE BARR SMITH LIBRARY

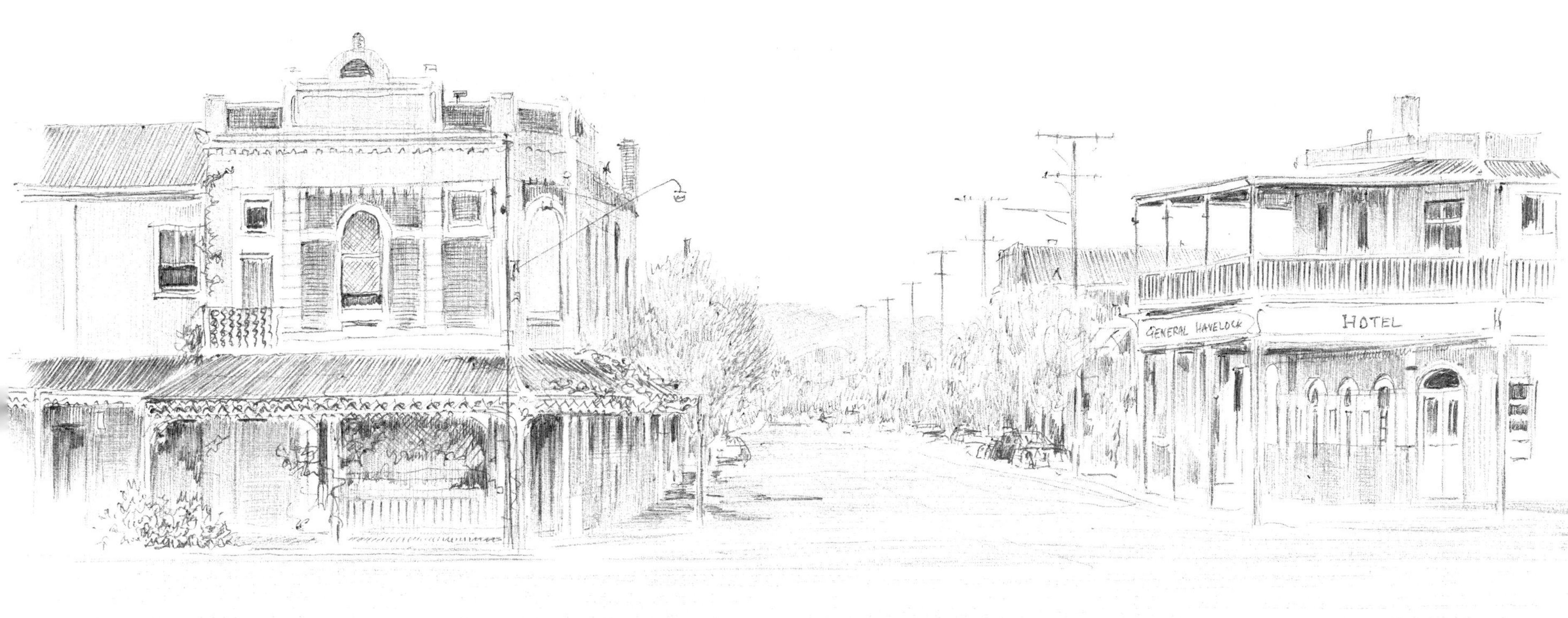

Hutt Street, Adelaide

Wide verandahs and wrought-iron lacework decorate many fine old bluestone buildings in the south-east corner of the city.

Barr Smith Library, University of Adelaide

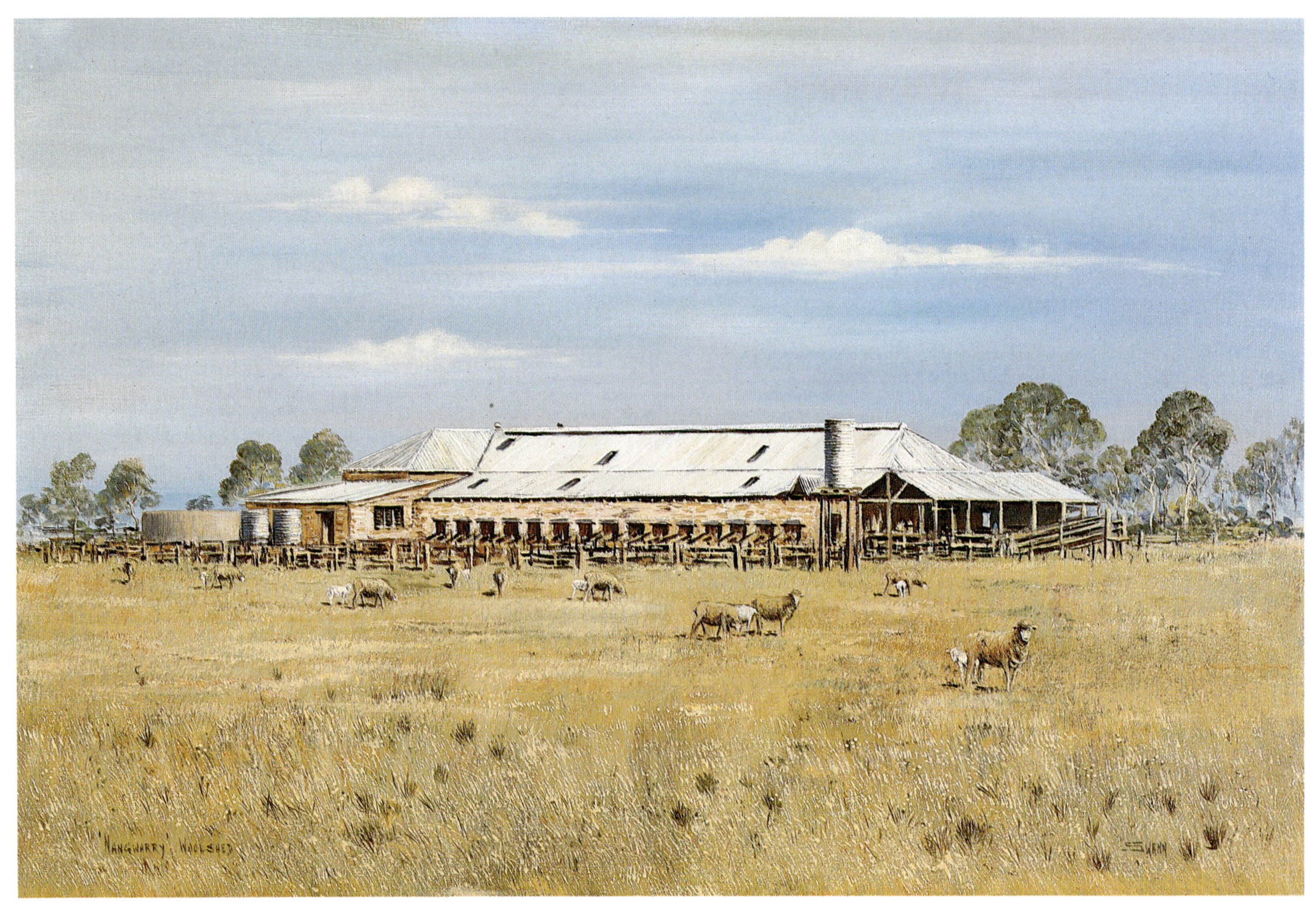

Nangwarry woolshed in the well-
watered South-East

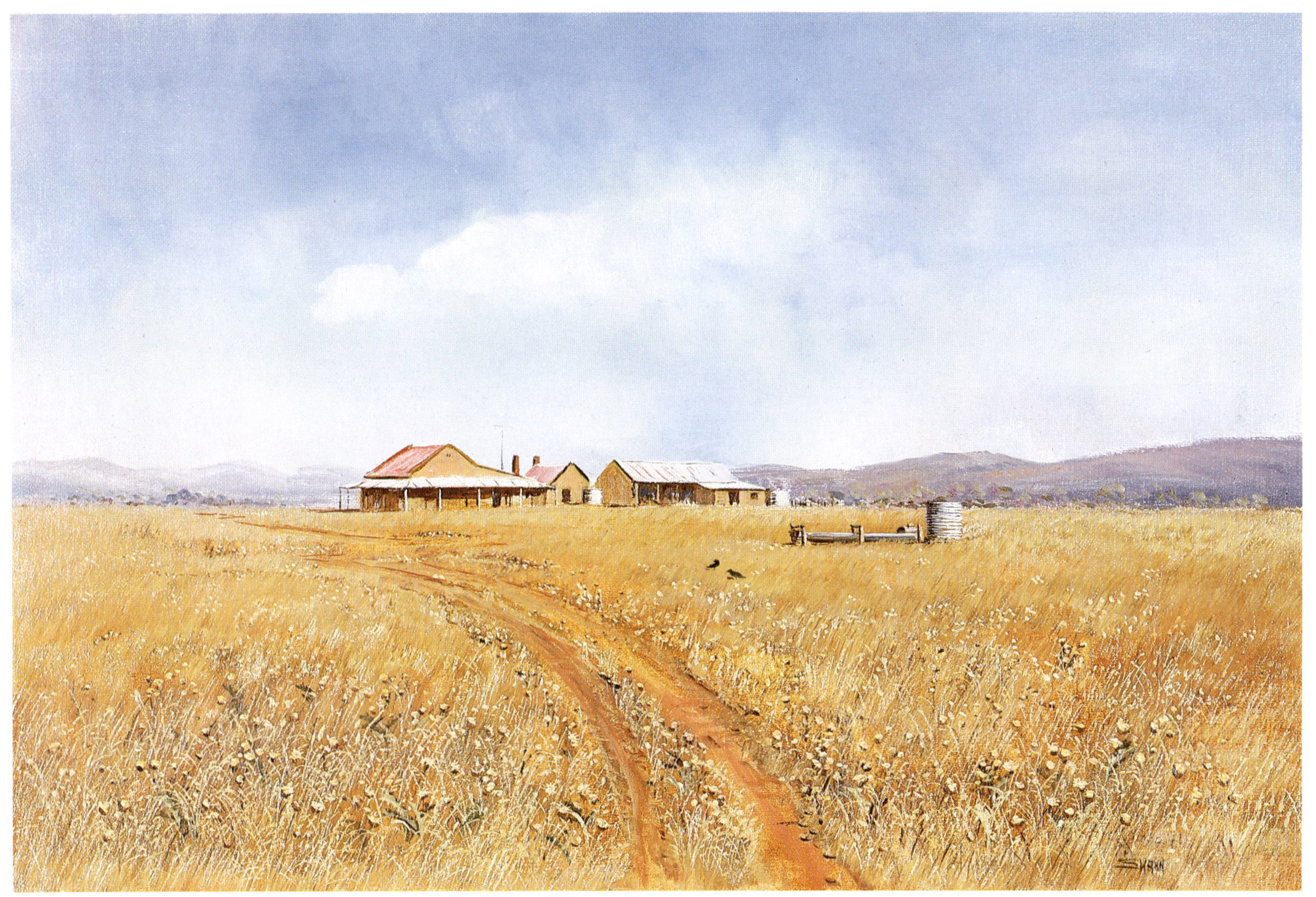

Northern homestead

Although dry, the north of the State is rich in colour: purple and blue hills, red soil, yellow grasses and clear blue skies stretch for thousands of kilometres.

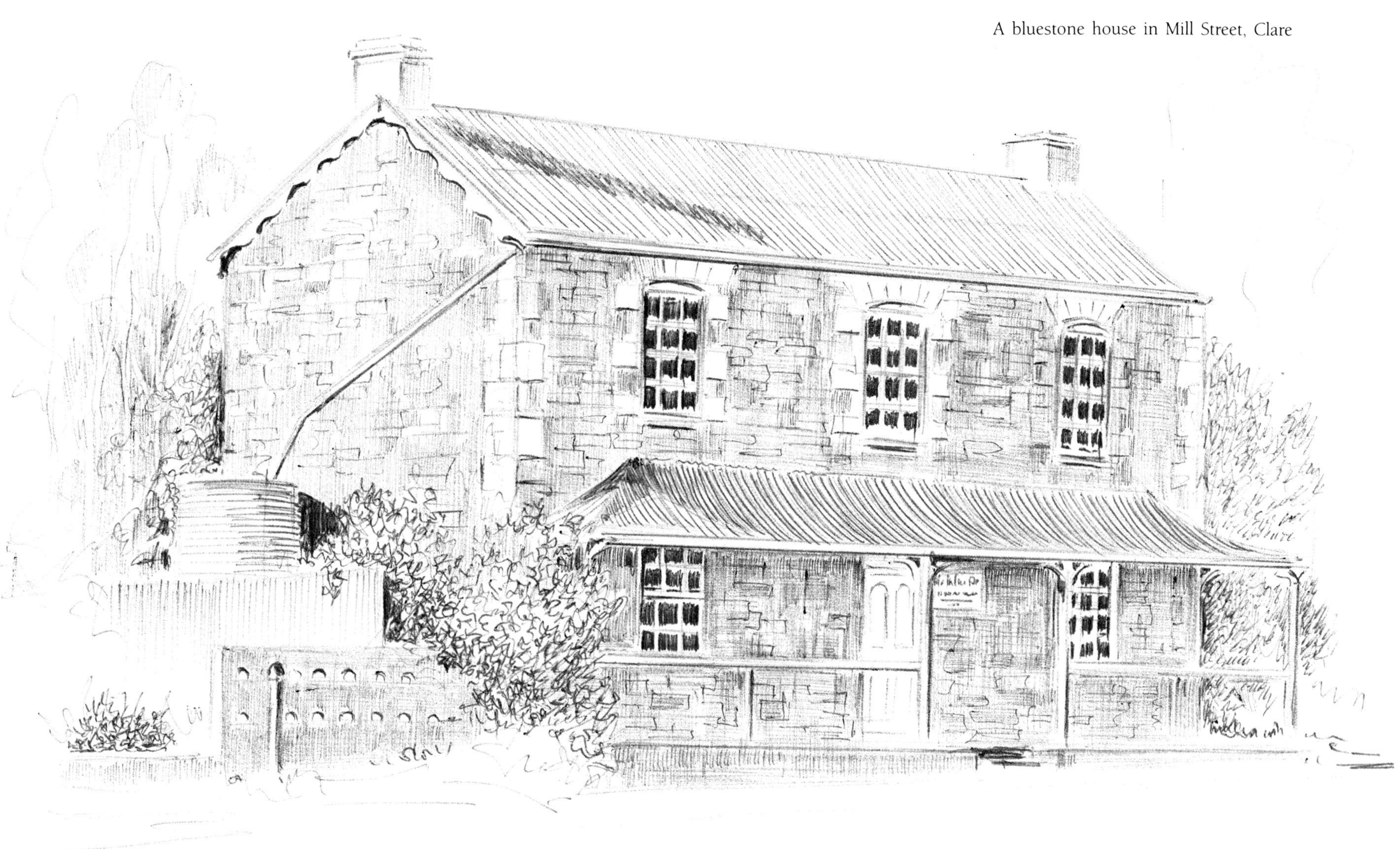

36

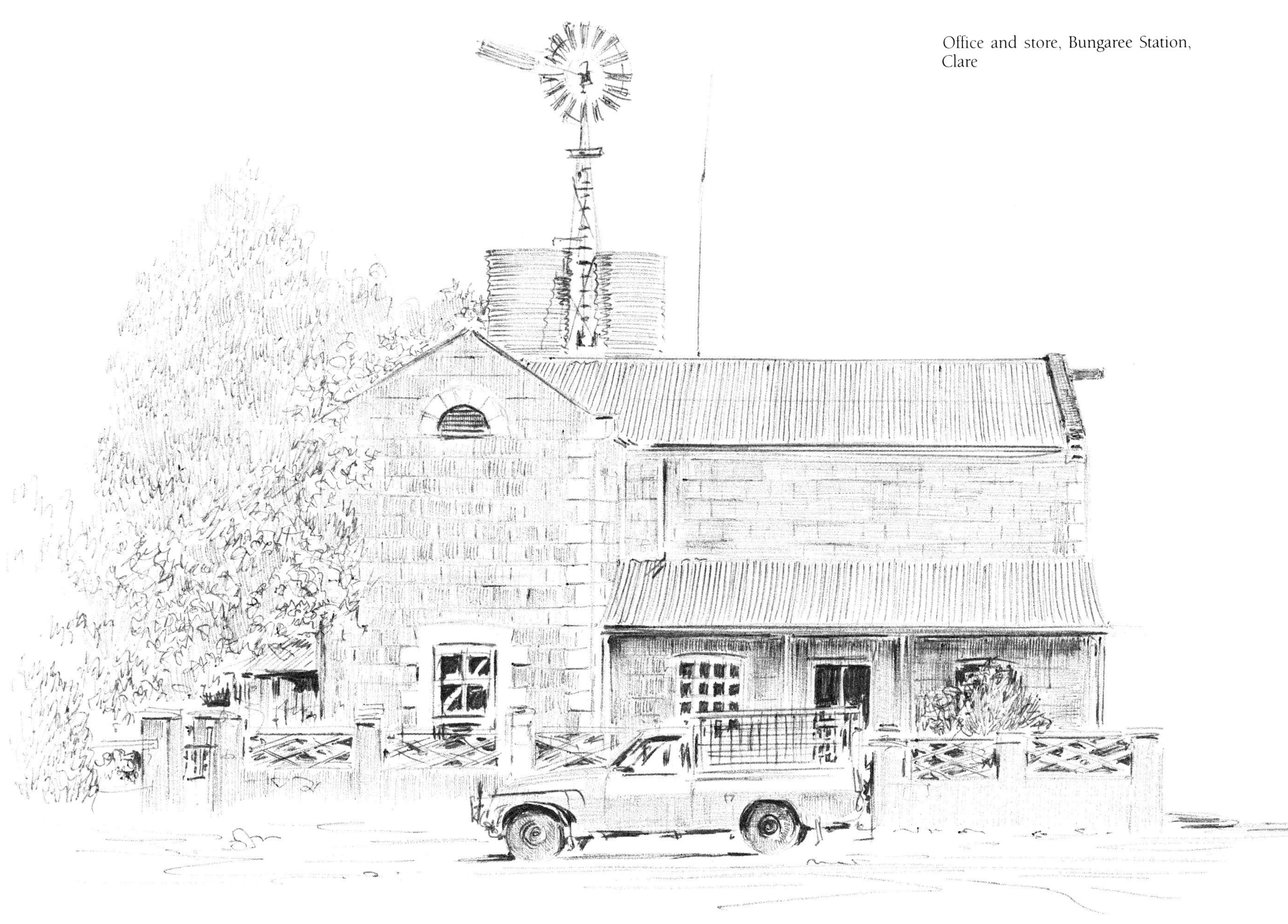

Office and store, Bungaree Station,
Clare

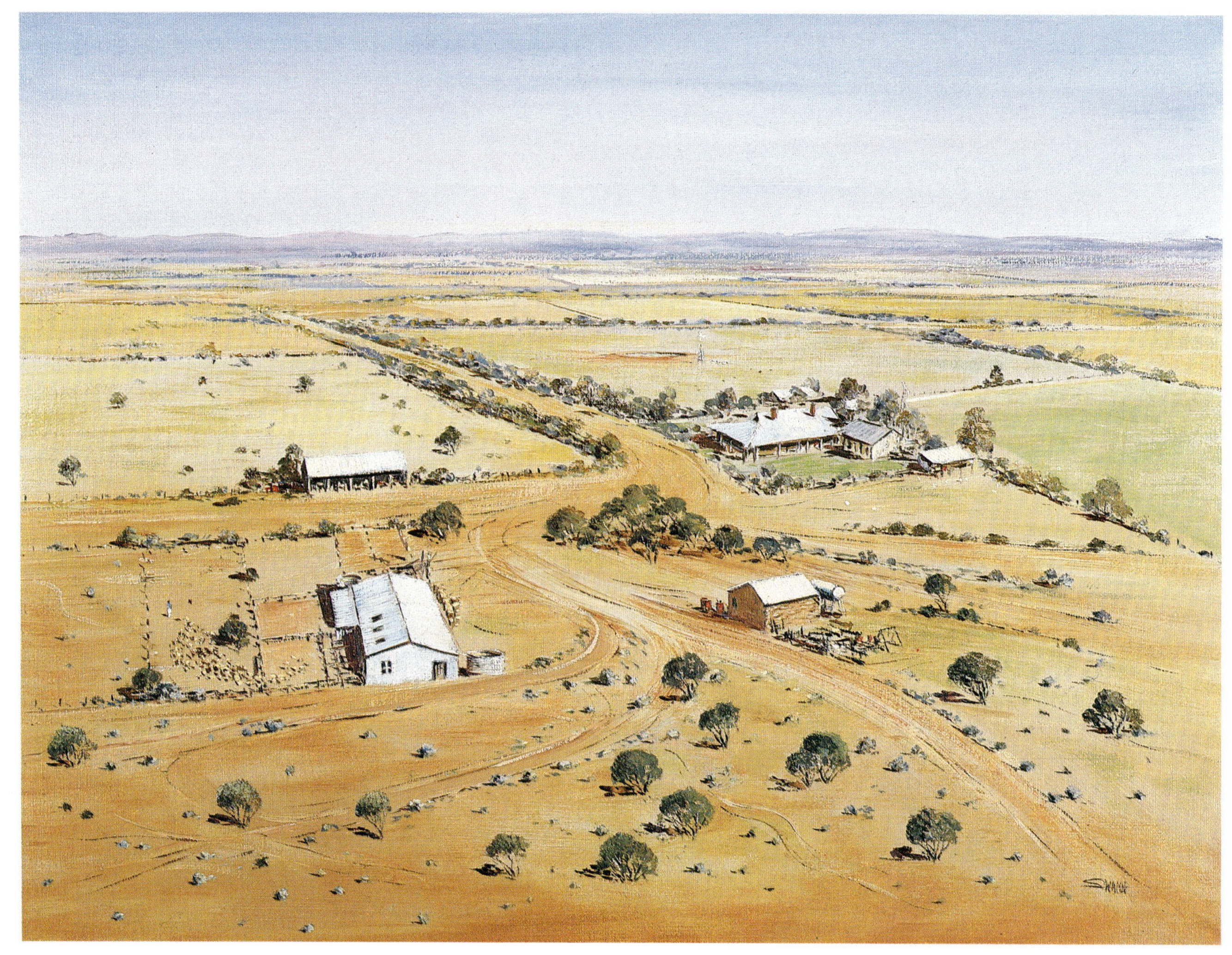

A mallee farm

*Sometimes I have used a light aircraft for
sketching trips. There is little time to capture
detail so the final painting is an impression
rather than an accurate record.*

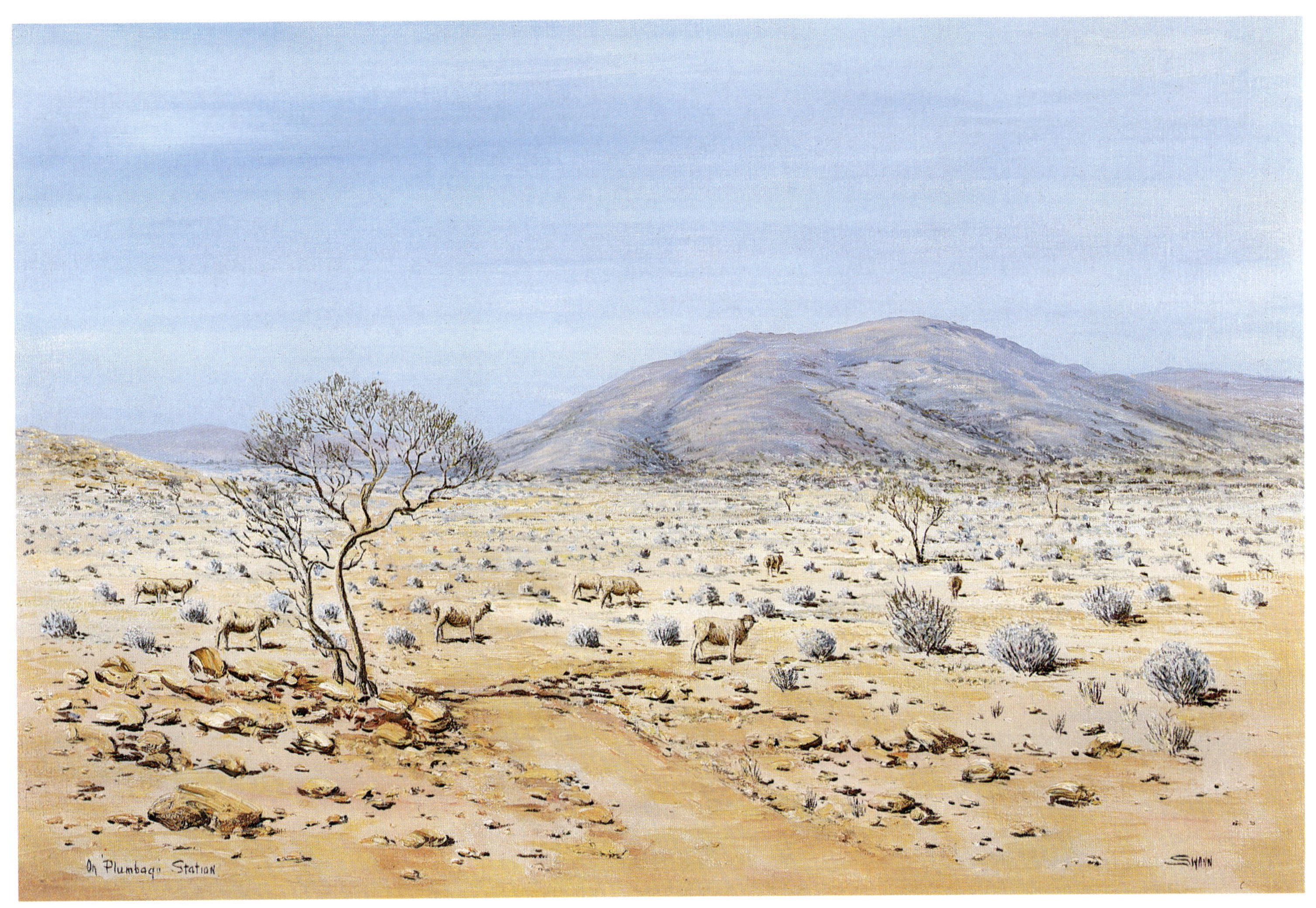

The Tombstone landmark on
Plumbago Station in the north-east

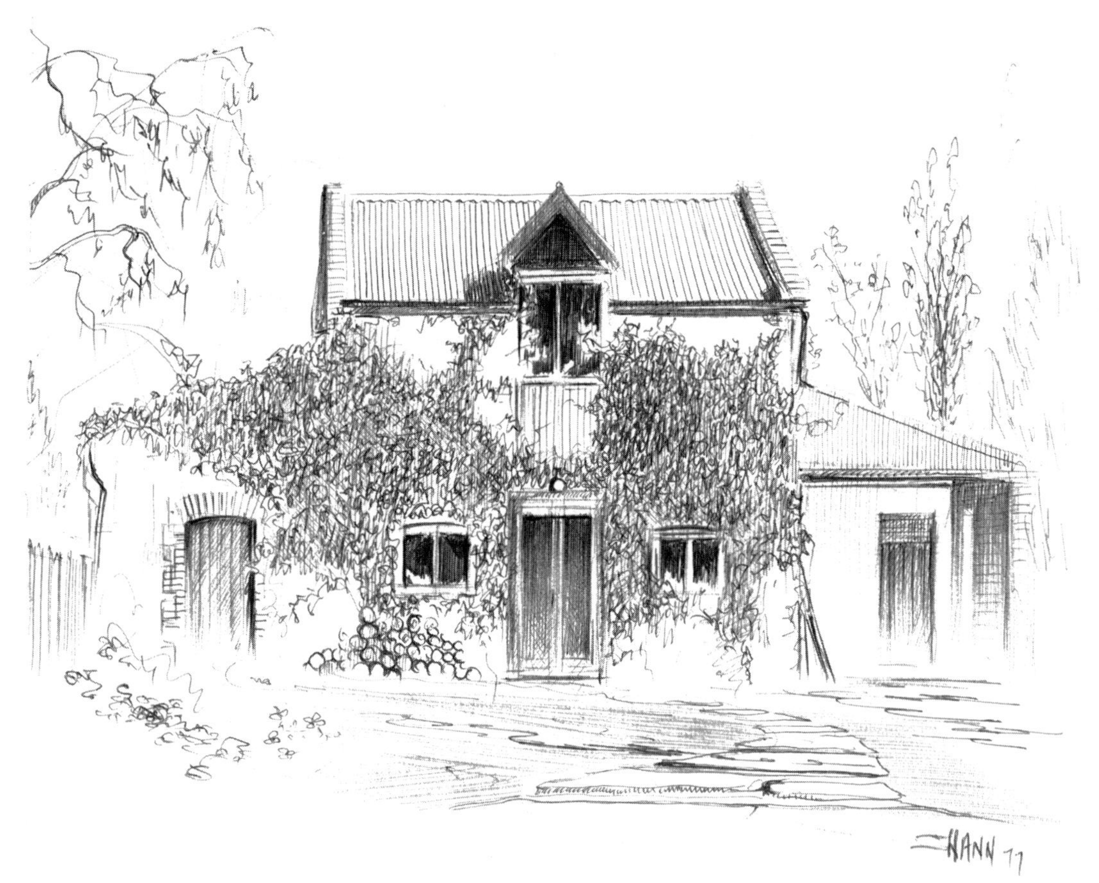

A stable and barn in North Adelaide
converted for use as an office

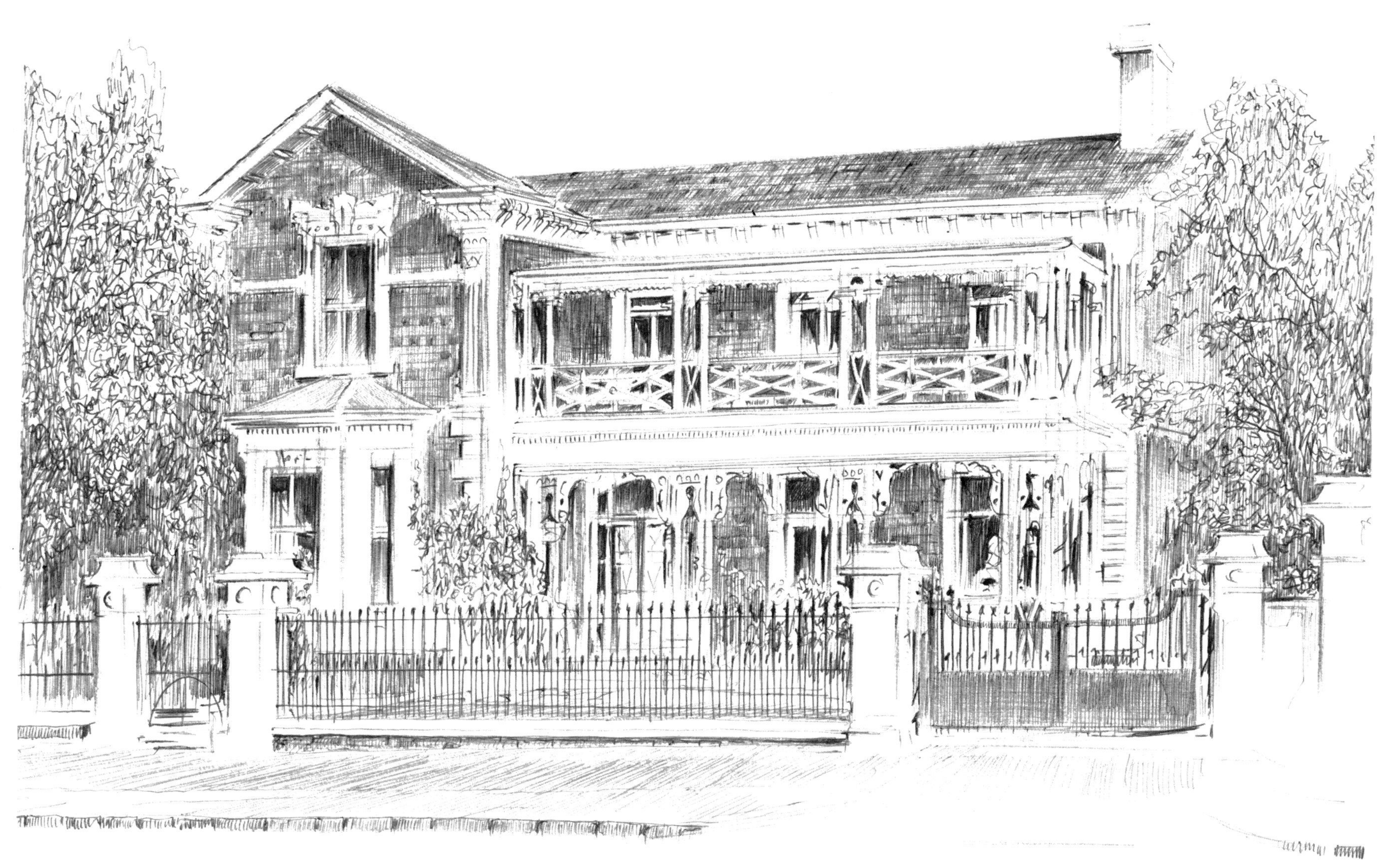

In Strangways Terrace, North Adelaide

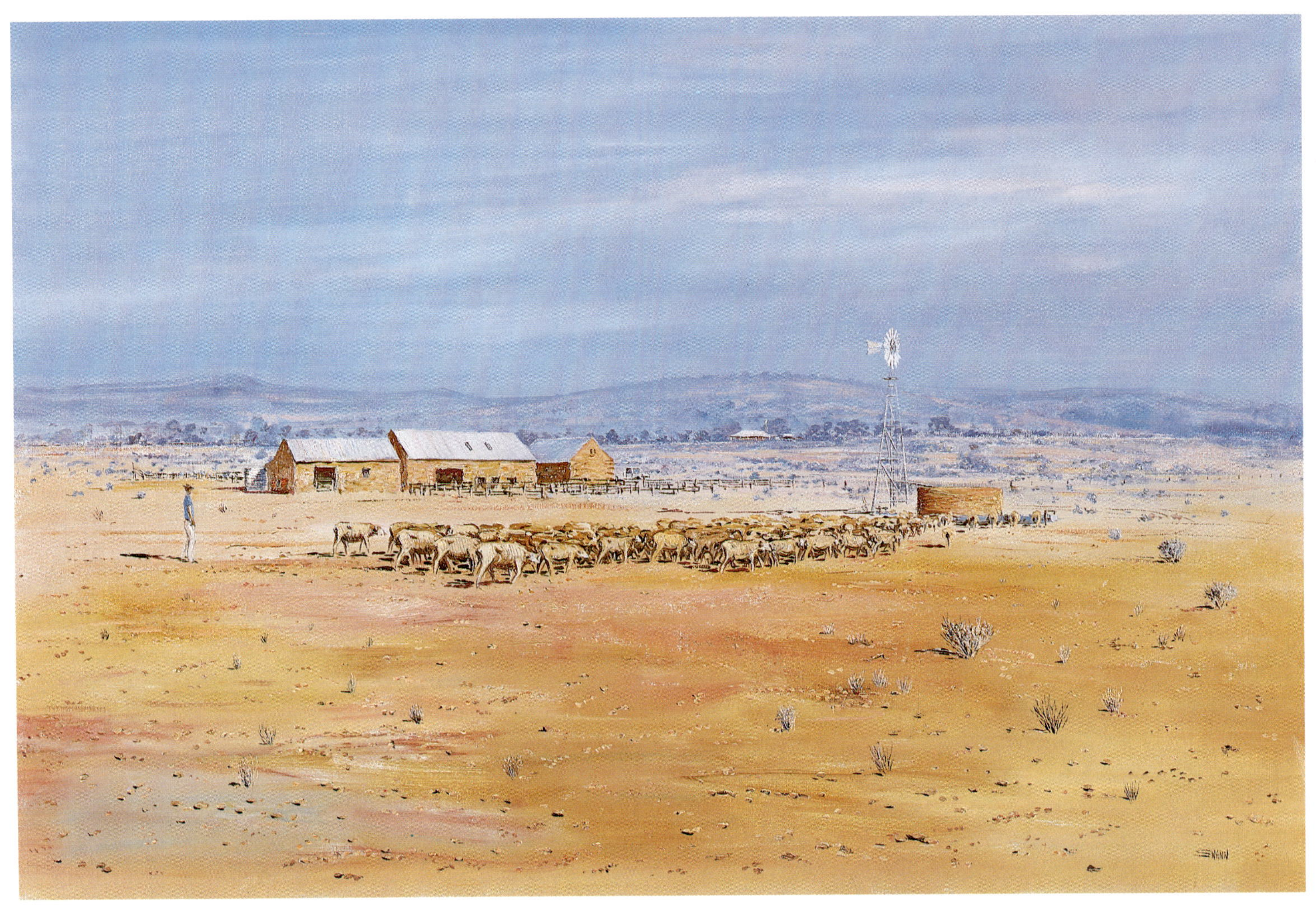

Northern wethers being yarded for
inspection before live export to the
Middle East

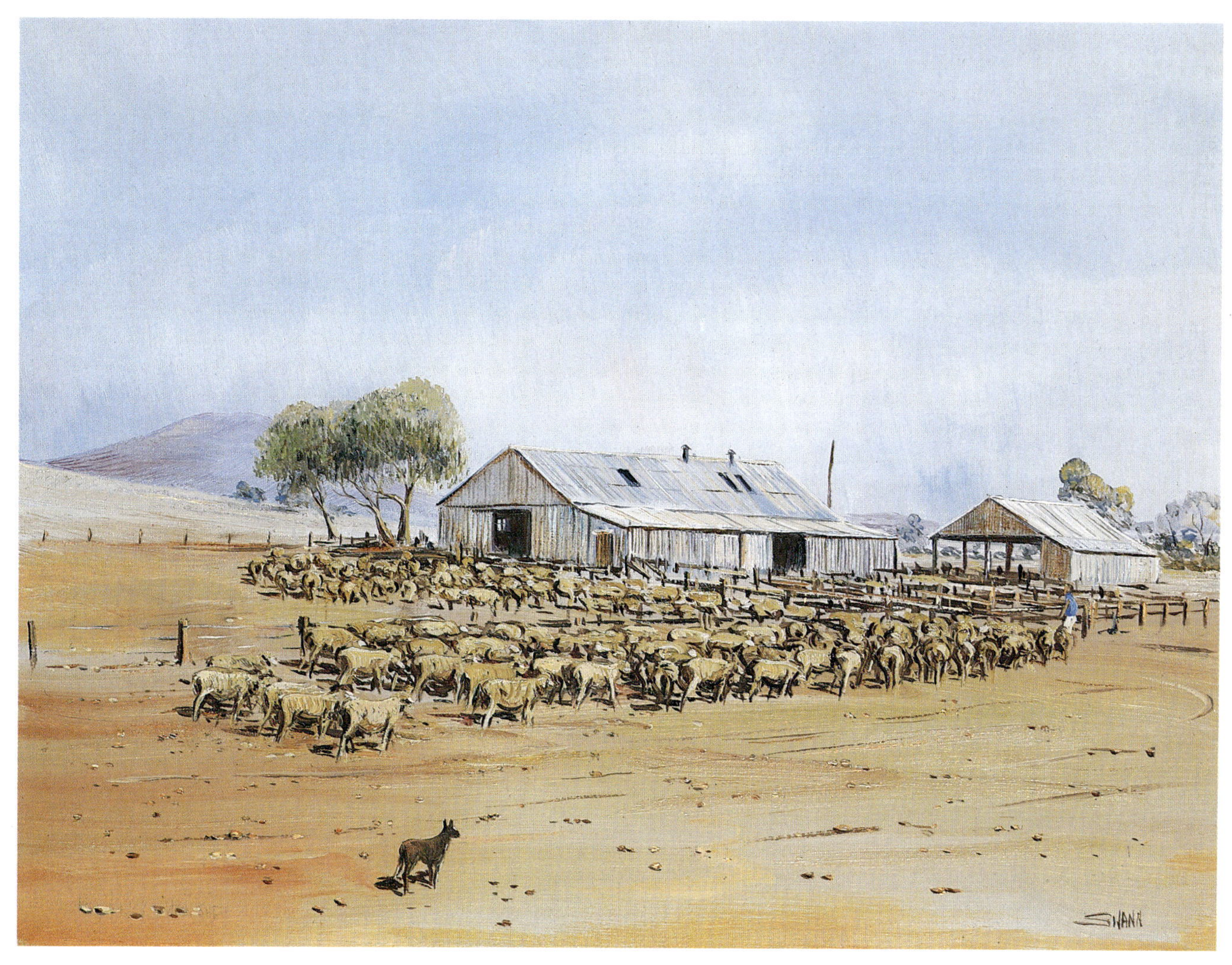

Millers' yards

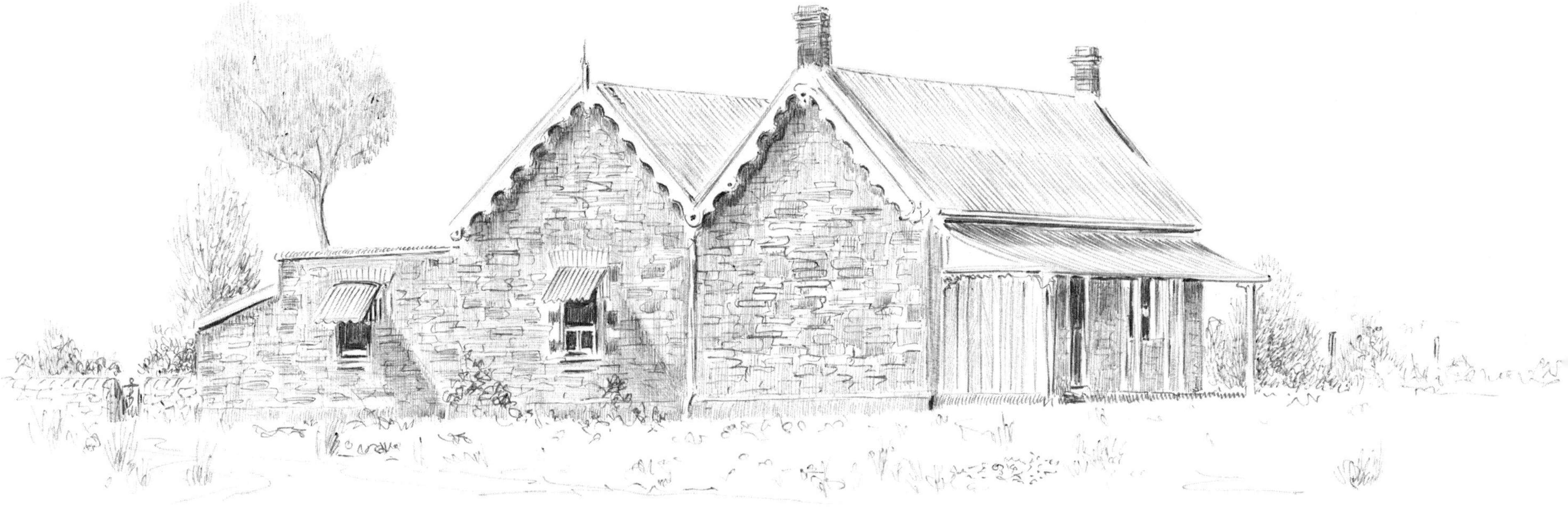

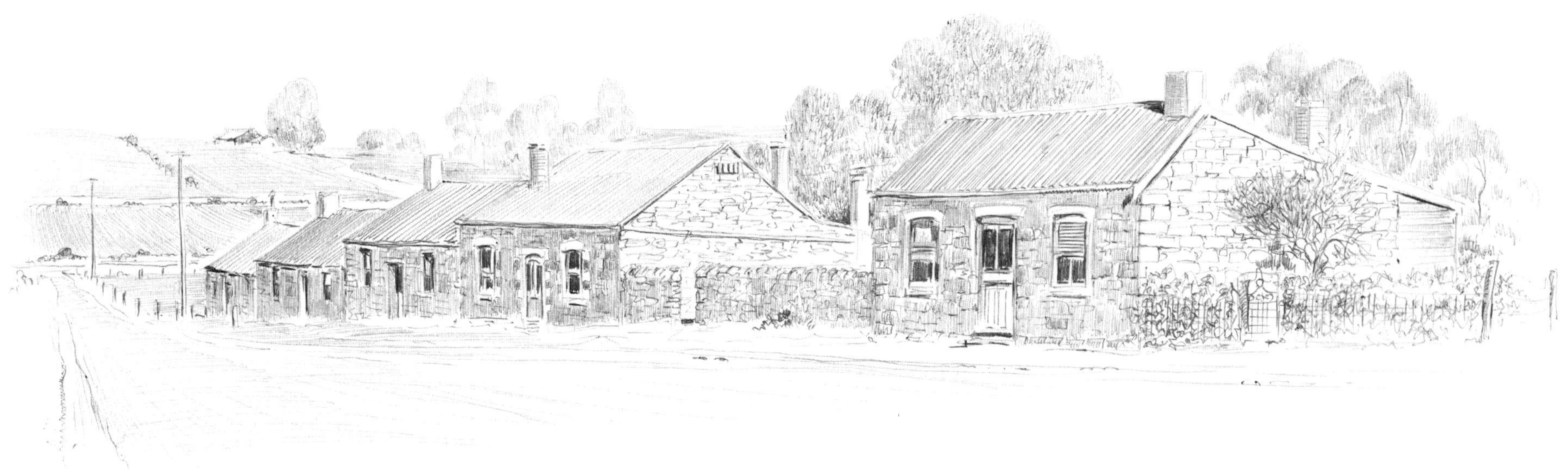

Miners' cottages at Burra Burra

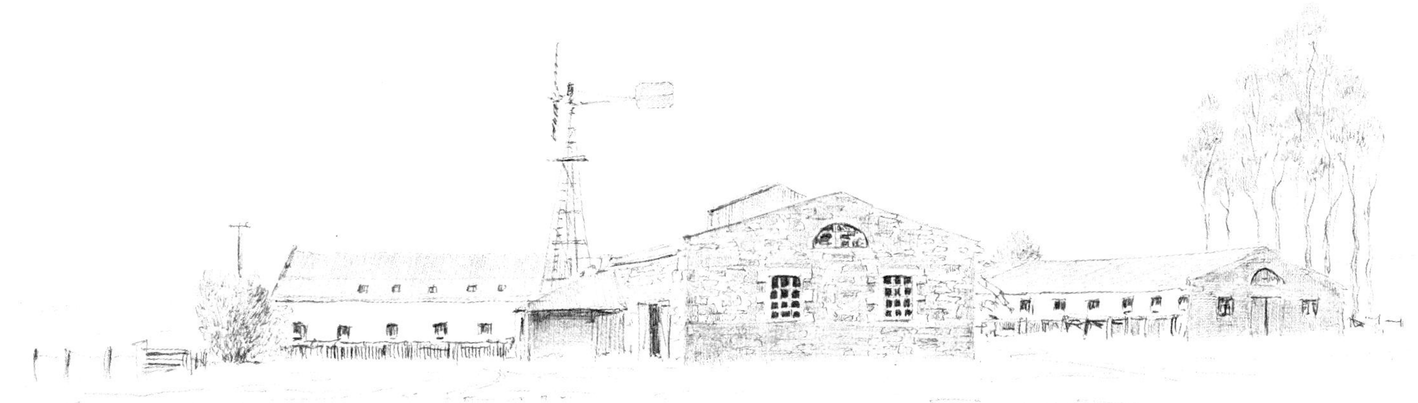

Bungaree woolshed, Clare

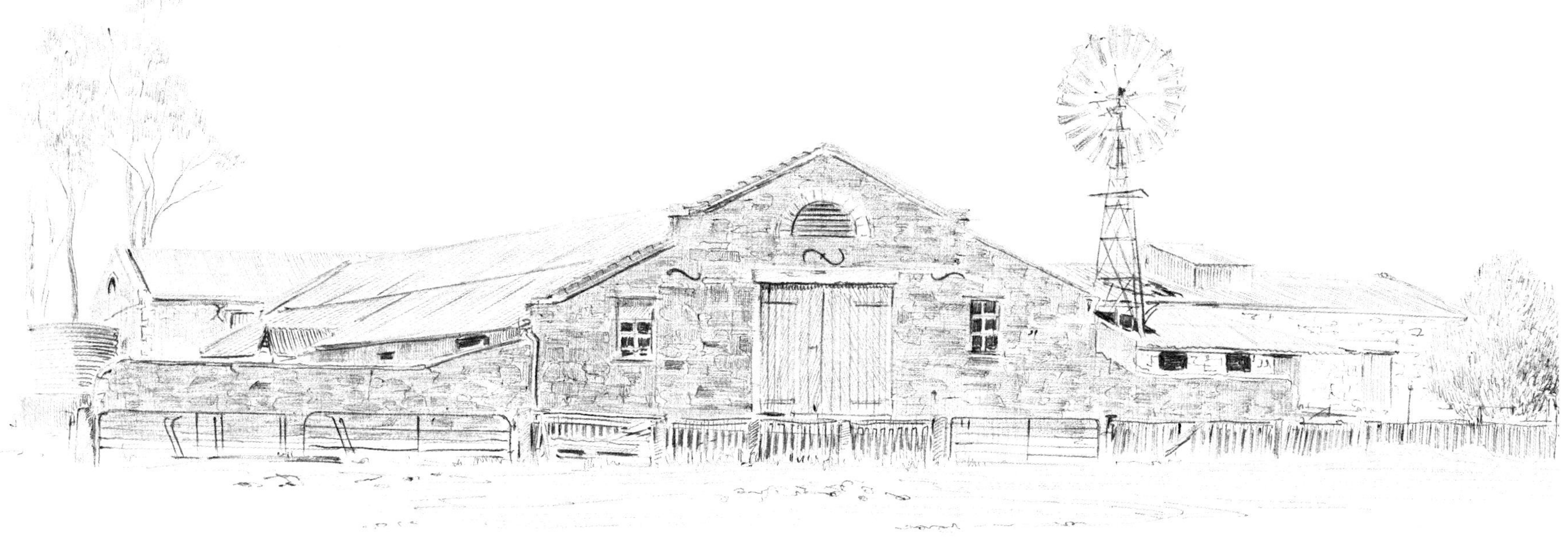

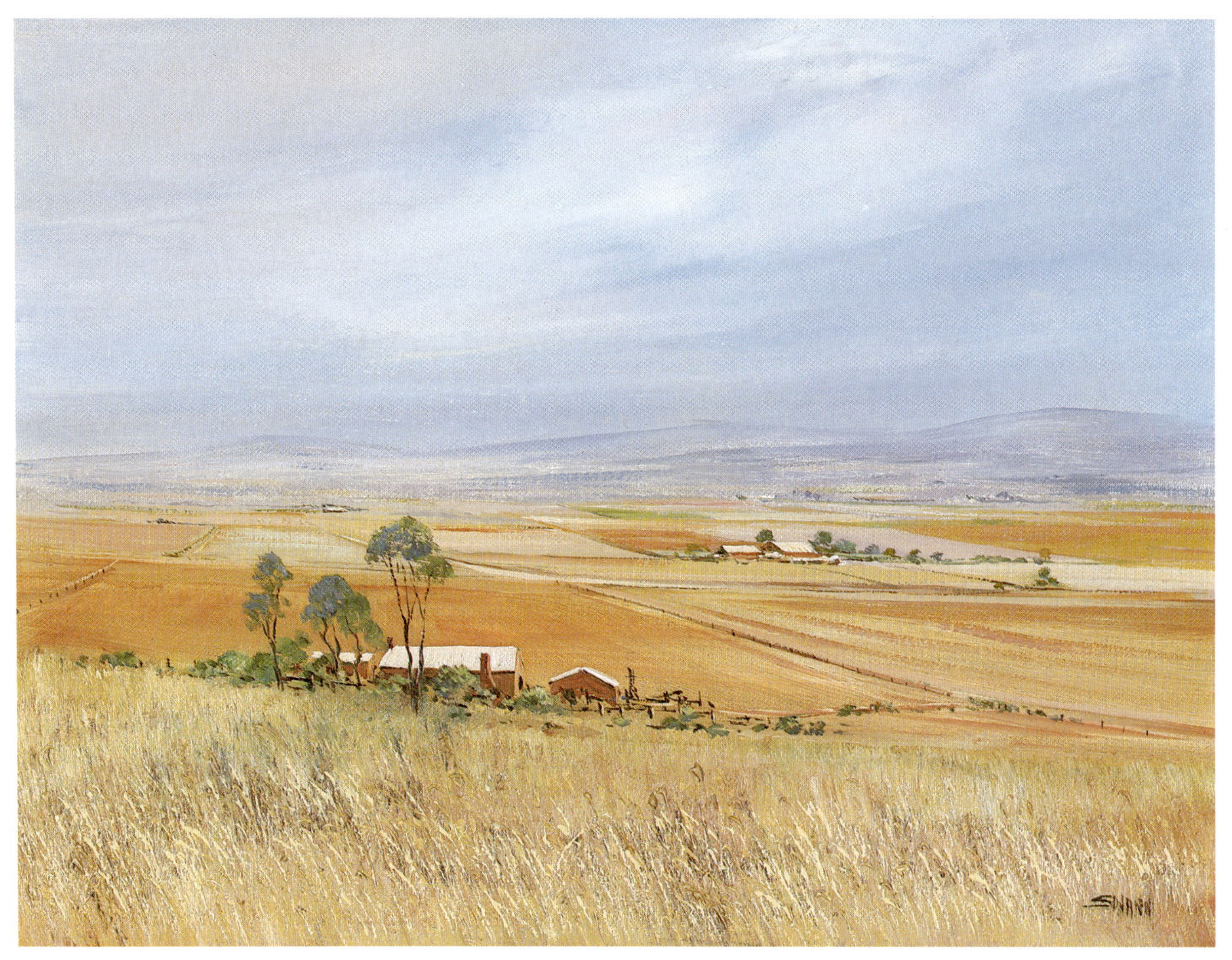

Fallow

*Sheep that are run on the red brown fallow
take on the same dusty colour as the
paddocks.*

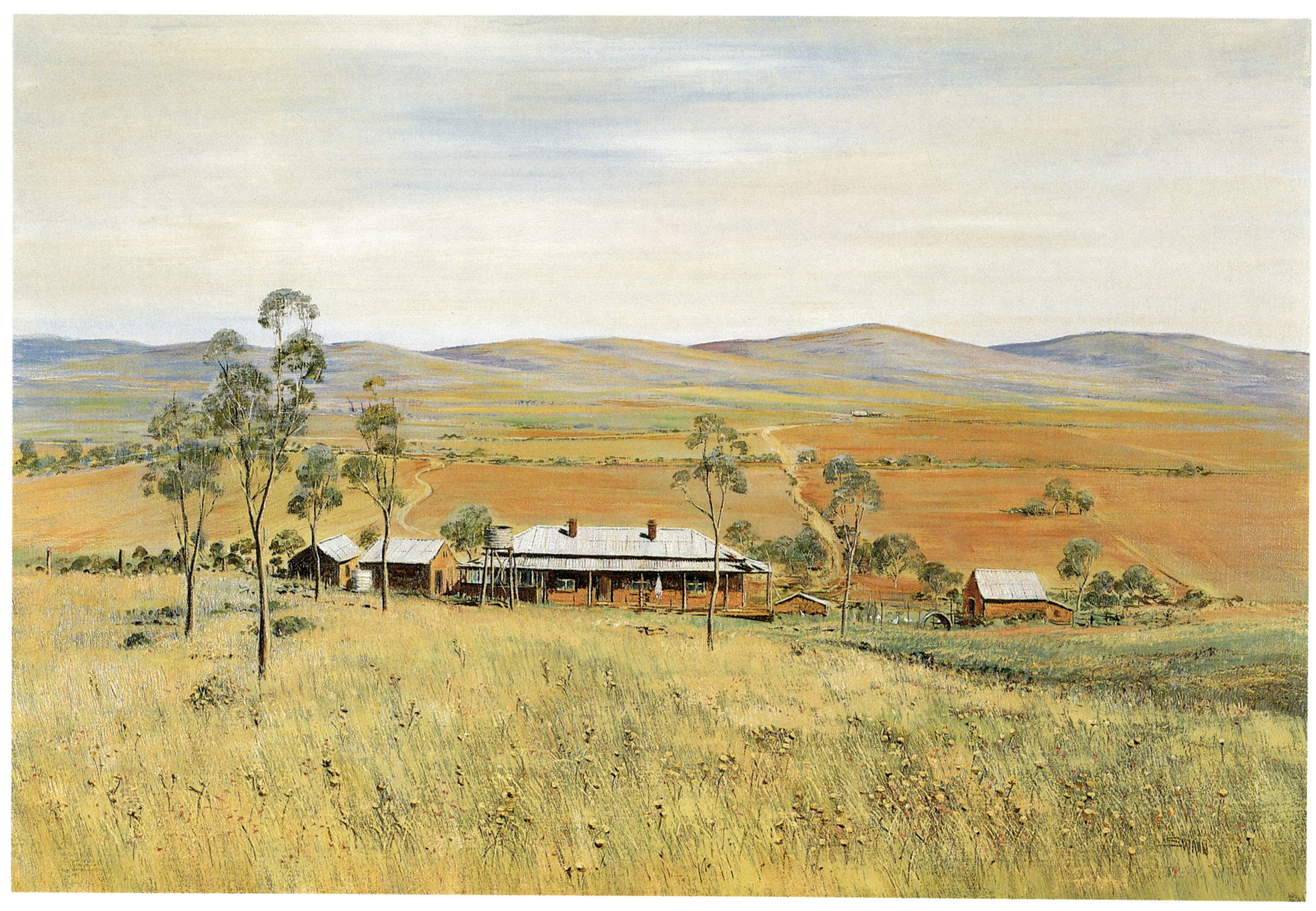

Fallow patterns

After the crops are harvested in late spring or early summer, the country is a pattern of brown and red fallow and yellow and brown stubble.

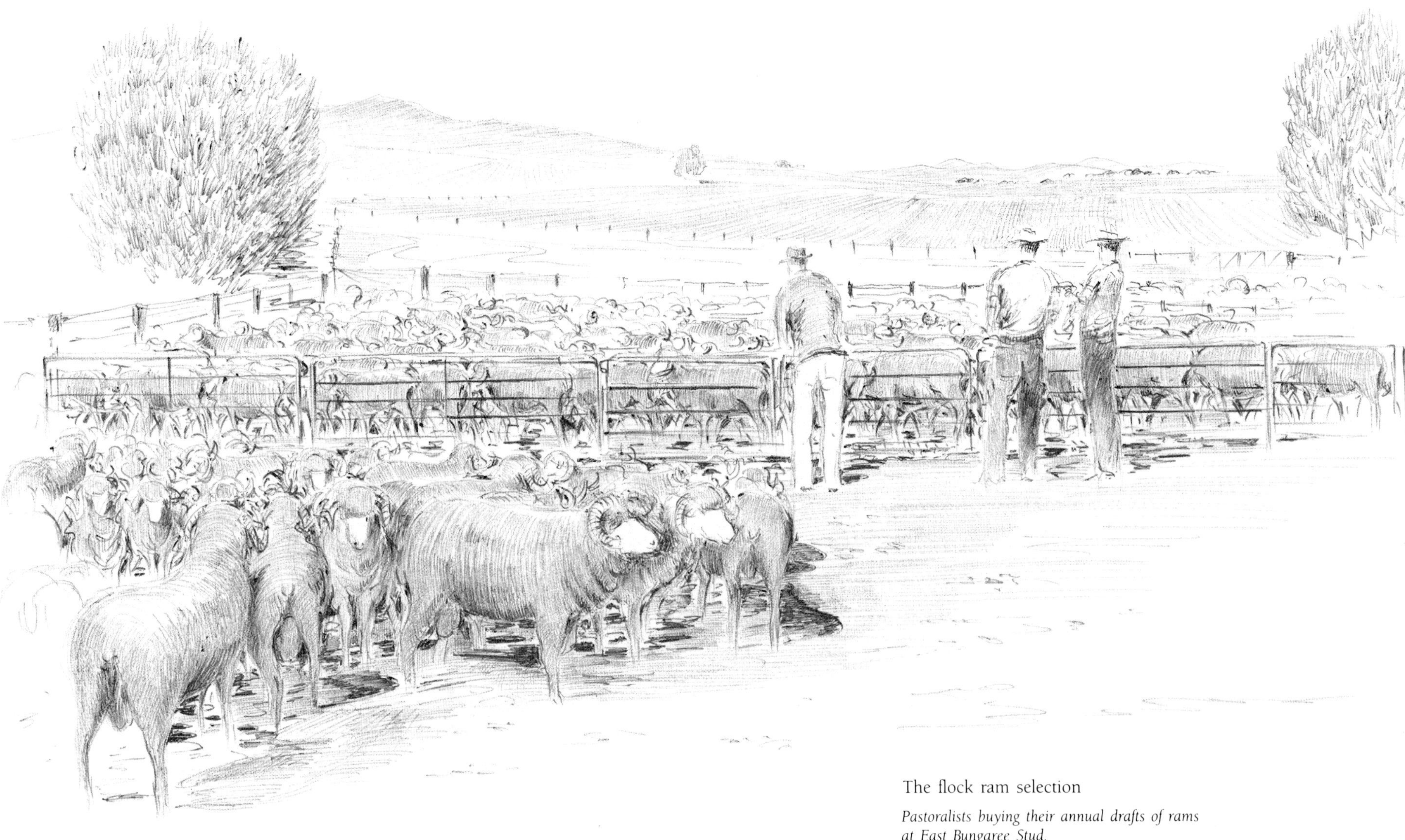

The flock ram selection

*Pastoralists buying their annual drafts of rams
at East Bungaree Stud.*

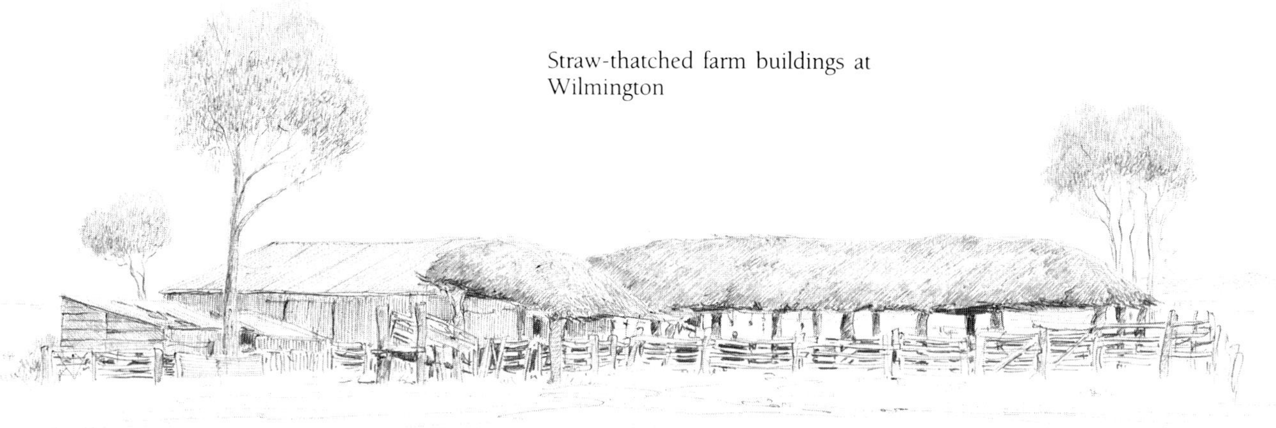

Straw-thatched farm buildings at
Wilmington

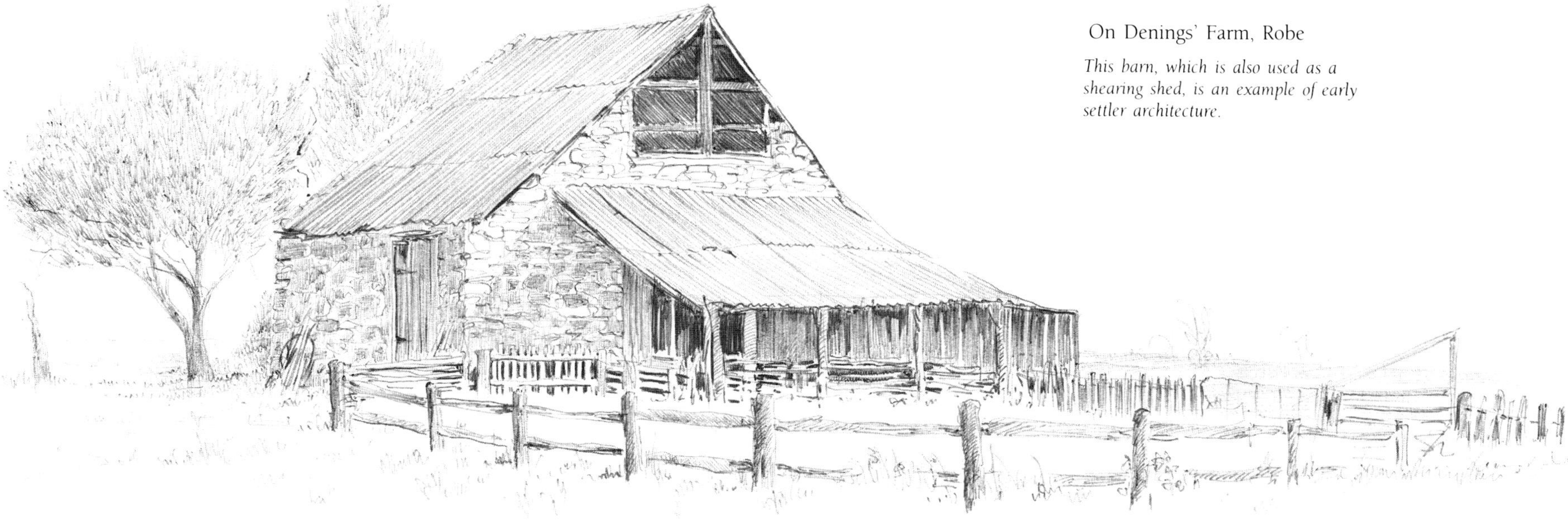

On Denings' Farm, Robe

*This barn, which is also used as a
shearing shed, is an example of early
settler architecture.*

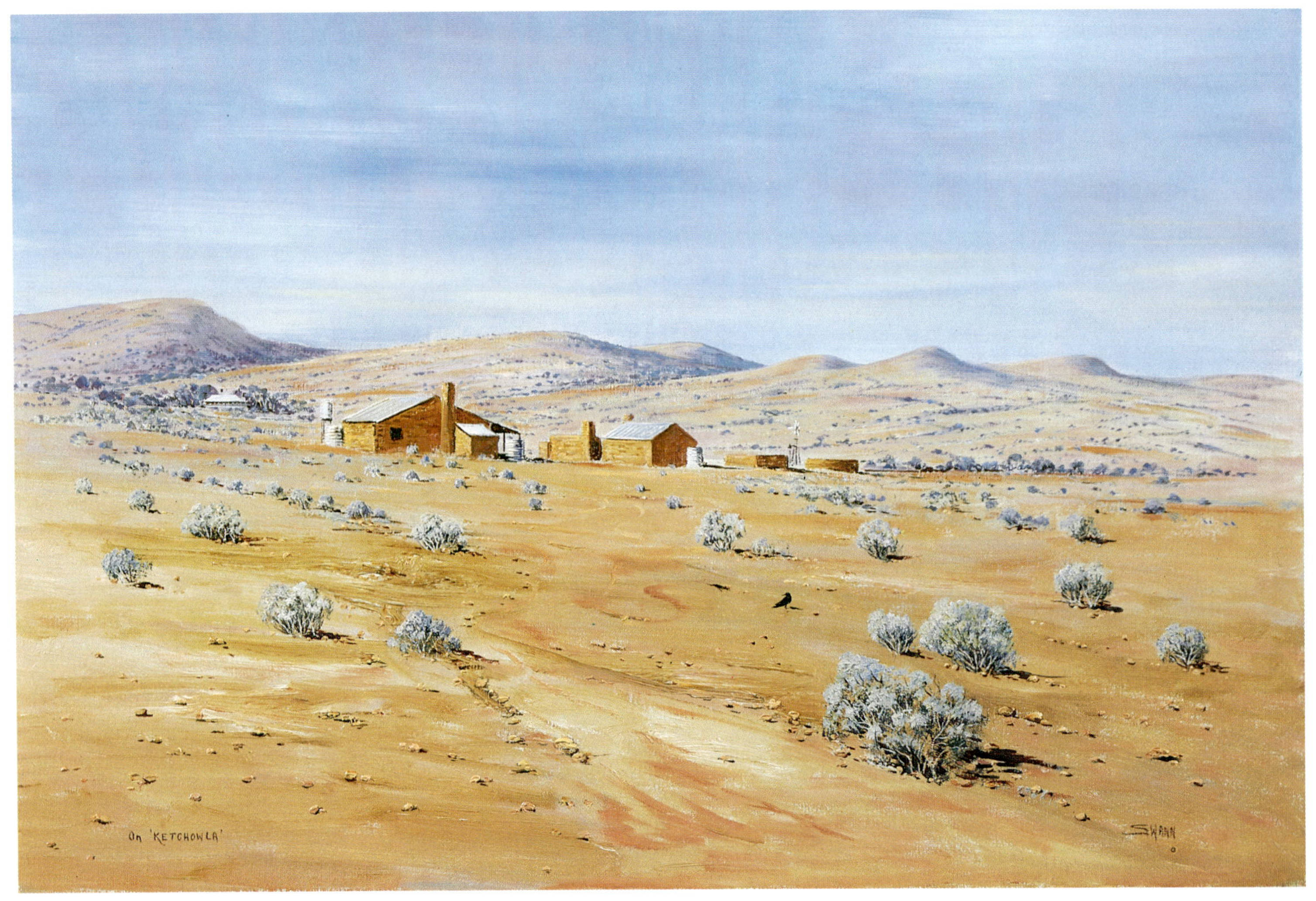

Shearers' quarters, Ketchowla Station

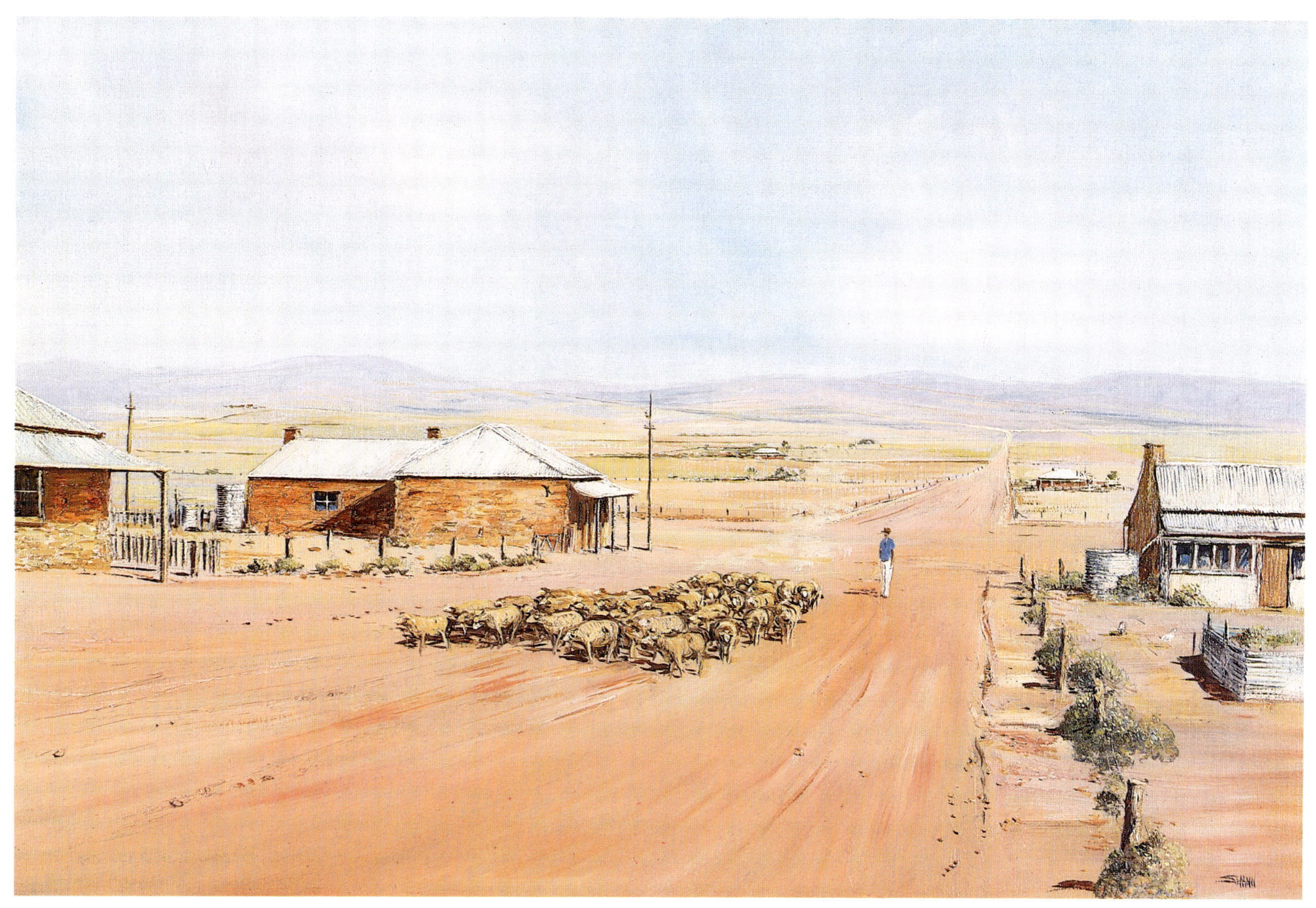

The quarter S van

*Using this mysterious title was irresistible.
Today most livestock is transported by road.
In my time, most was consigned by rail. A
sheep van held about 200 sheep. For a small
lot of fifty, one ordered a quarter S van.*

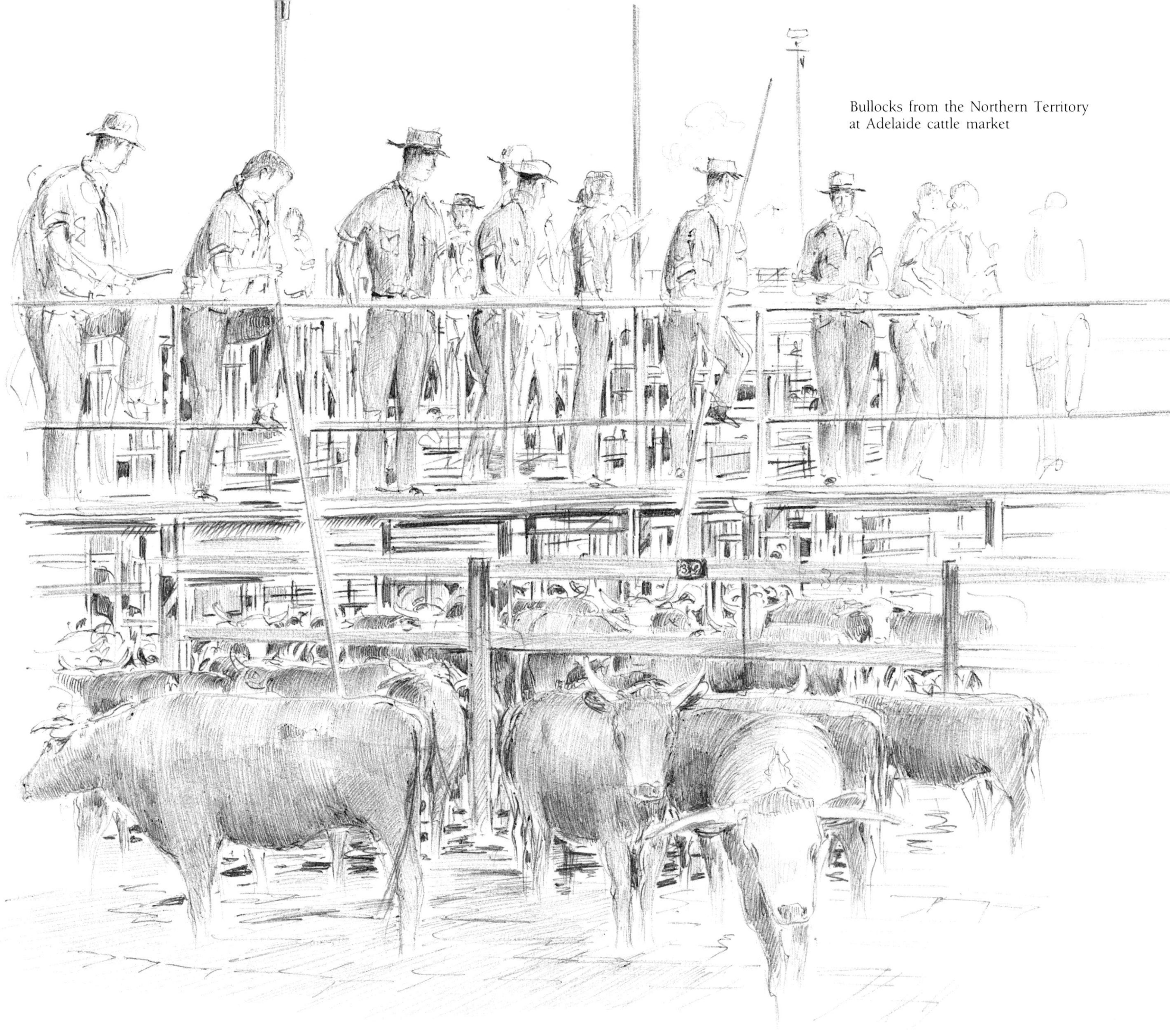

Bullocks from the Northern Territory
at Adelaide cattle market

At the cattle market

*Stockmen up early to draft cattle for the day's
sale.*

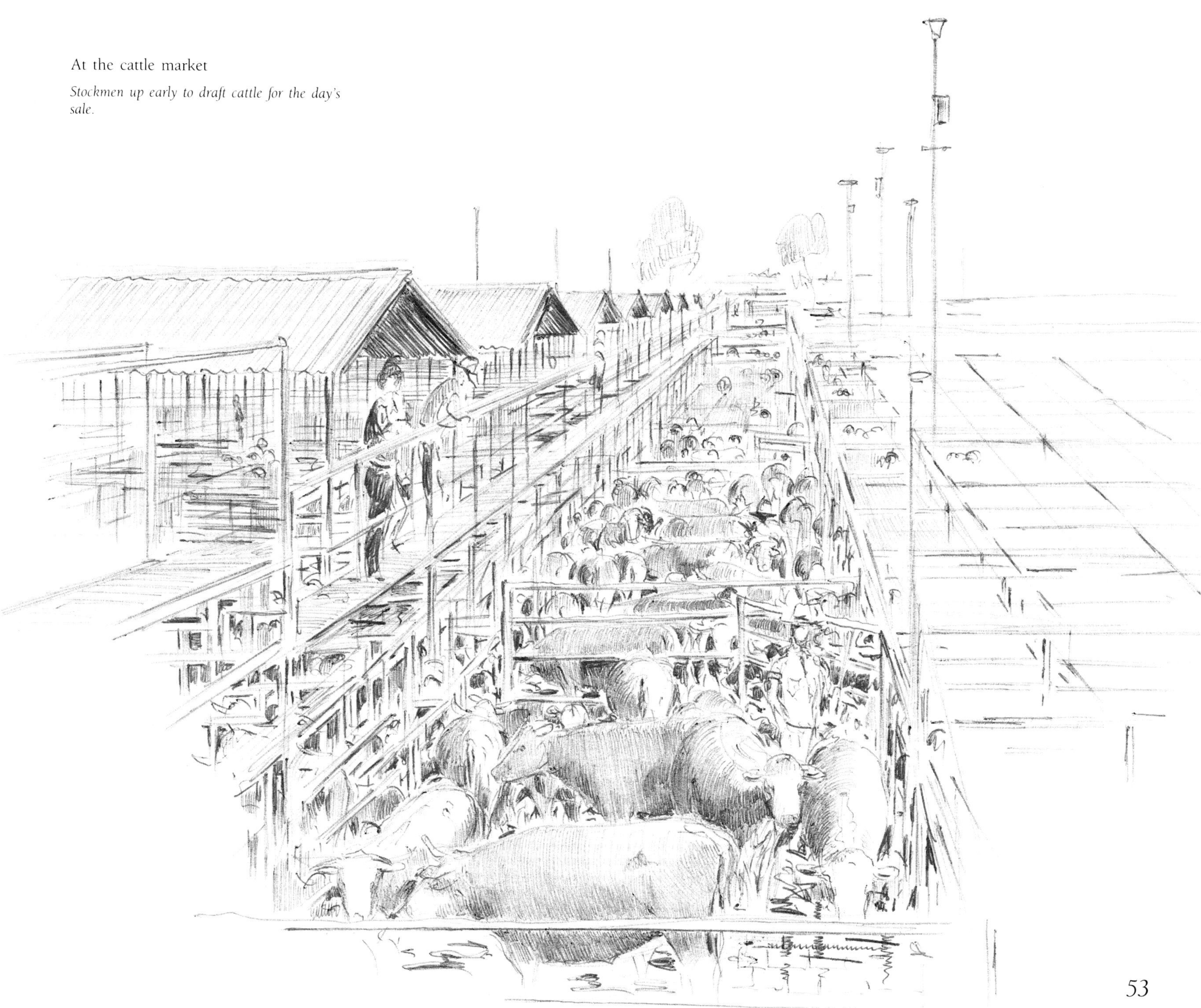

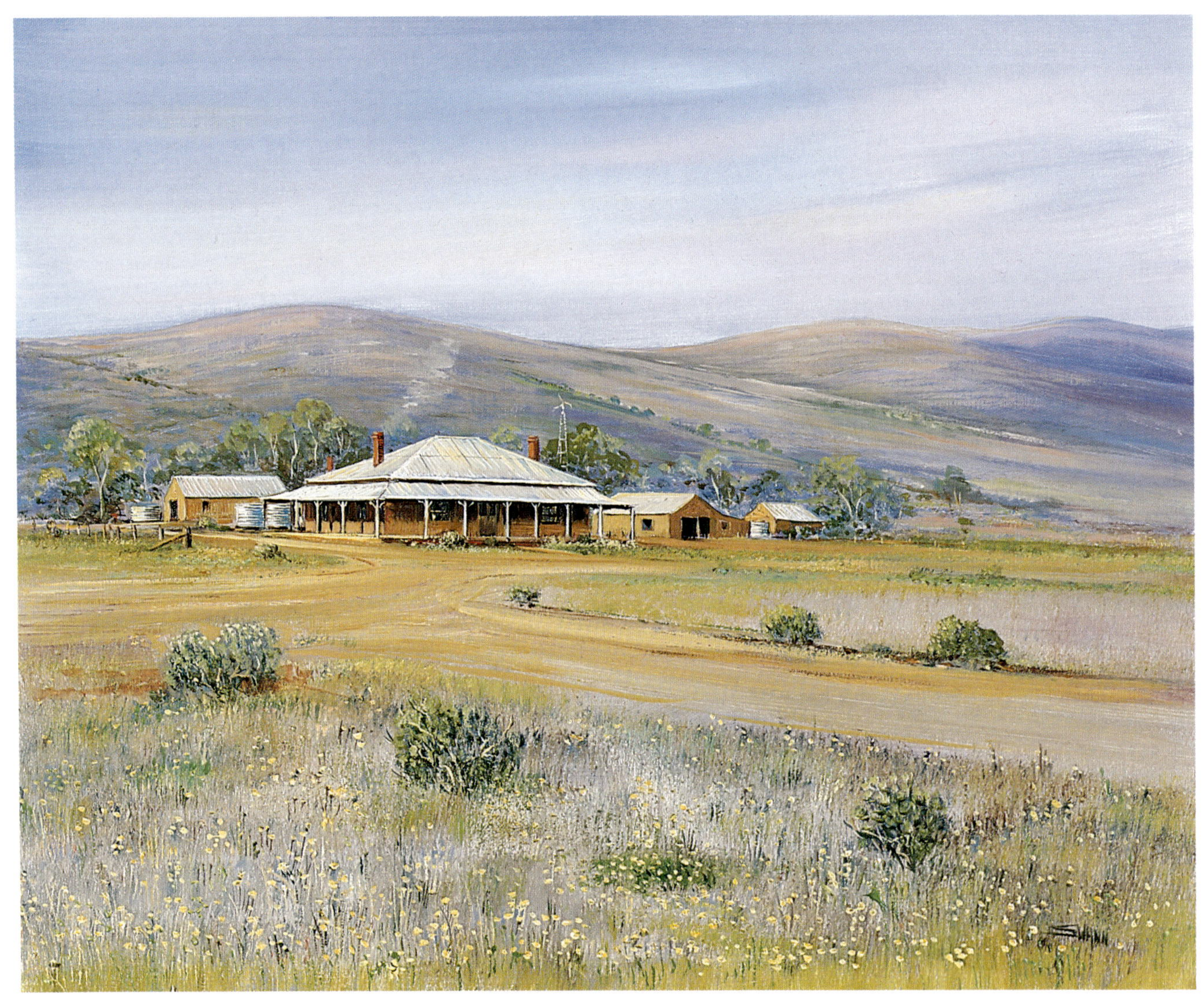

The Lighting plant

*Main power and generators have replaced
most of the wind-driven plants. However,
years ago farmers and graziers relied on tall
towers, propellers and a good wind to
generate electricity.*

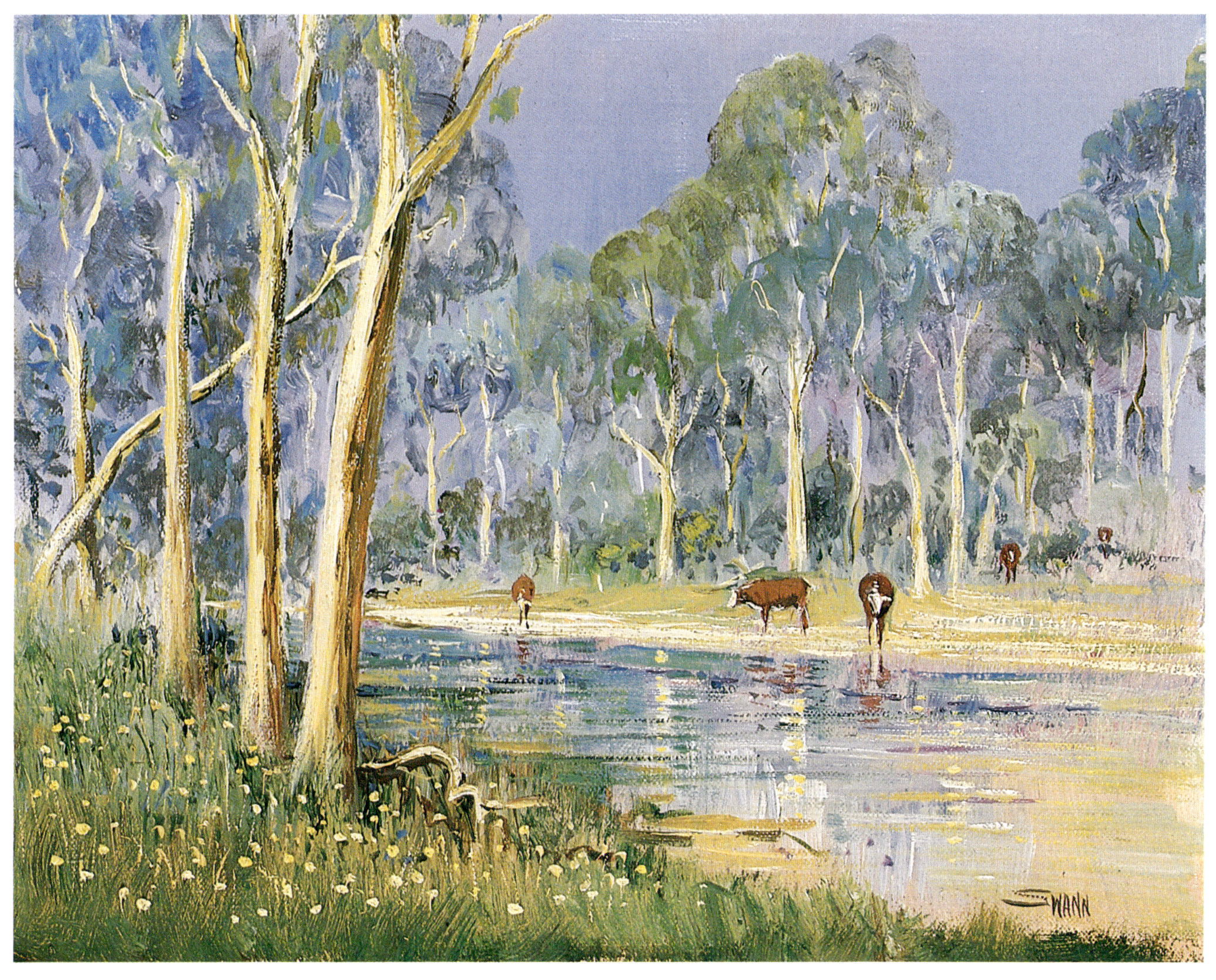

Evening drink at Yerelina Creek,
Strzelecki Track

Denings' Farm, Robe

*Built on the outskirts of Robe in 1851.
In the stillness of the night, the wind in
the sheoaks sounds like distant surf.*

Main Street, Callington

*This tiny township lies on the eastern
slopes of the Mount Lofty Ranges. Many
of its buildings are in the richly coloured
local stone used extensively by early
settlers.*

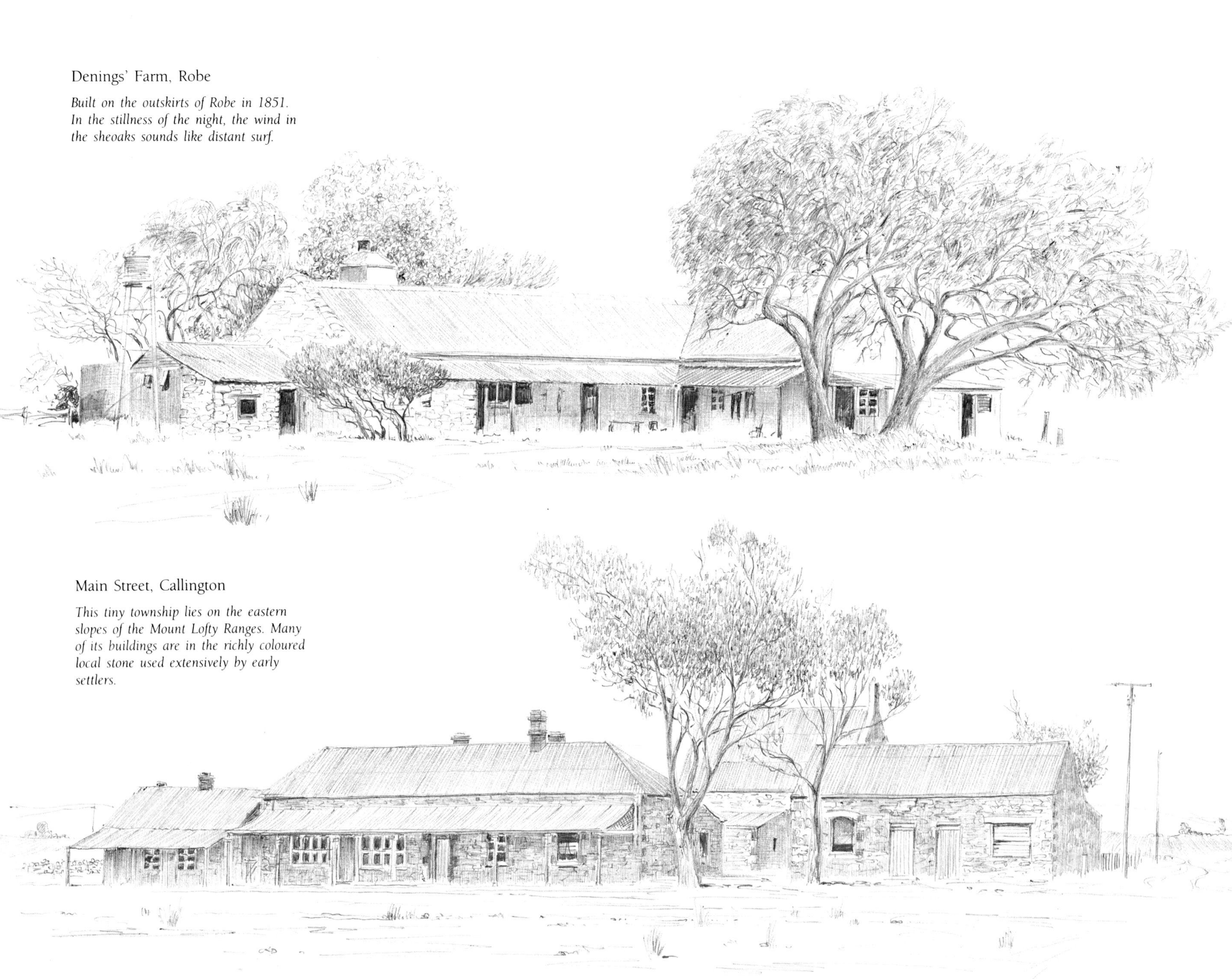

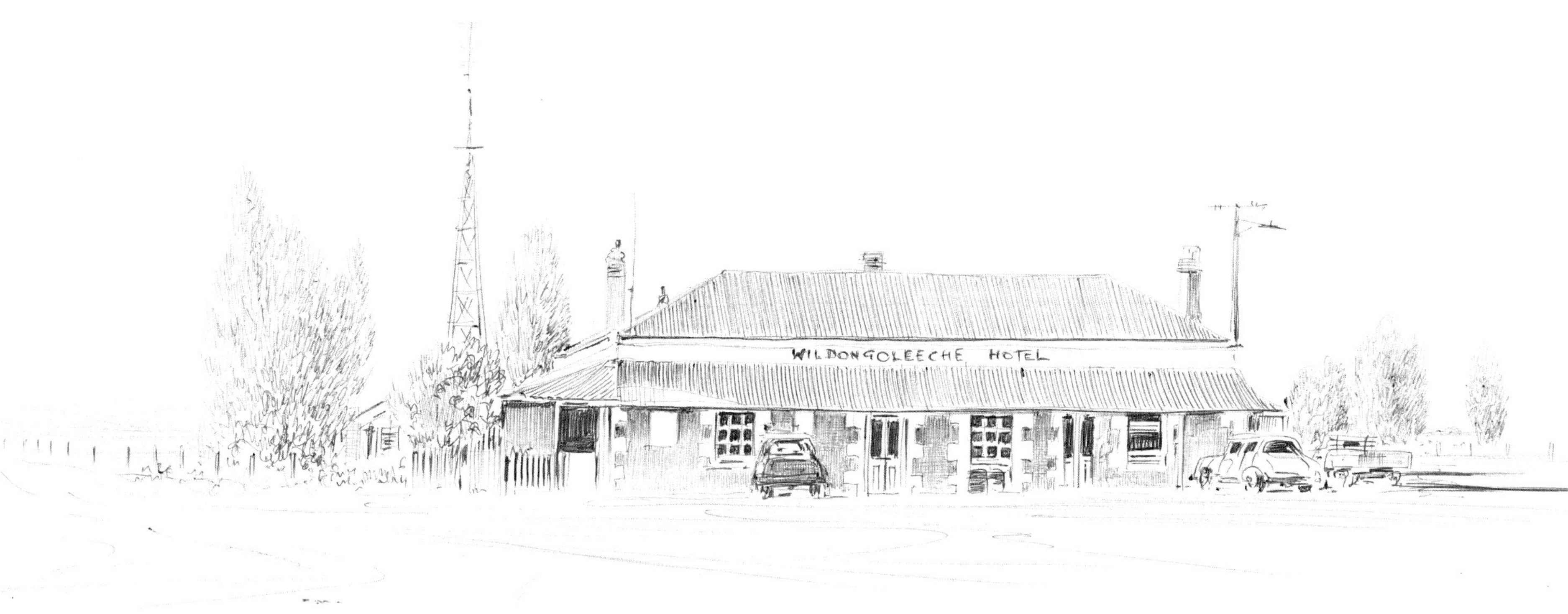

'The Wild Dog'

The only hotel in Hallett. The pub is a well-known meeting place for stud breeders, stock agents and graziers.

57

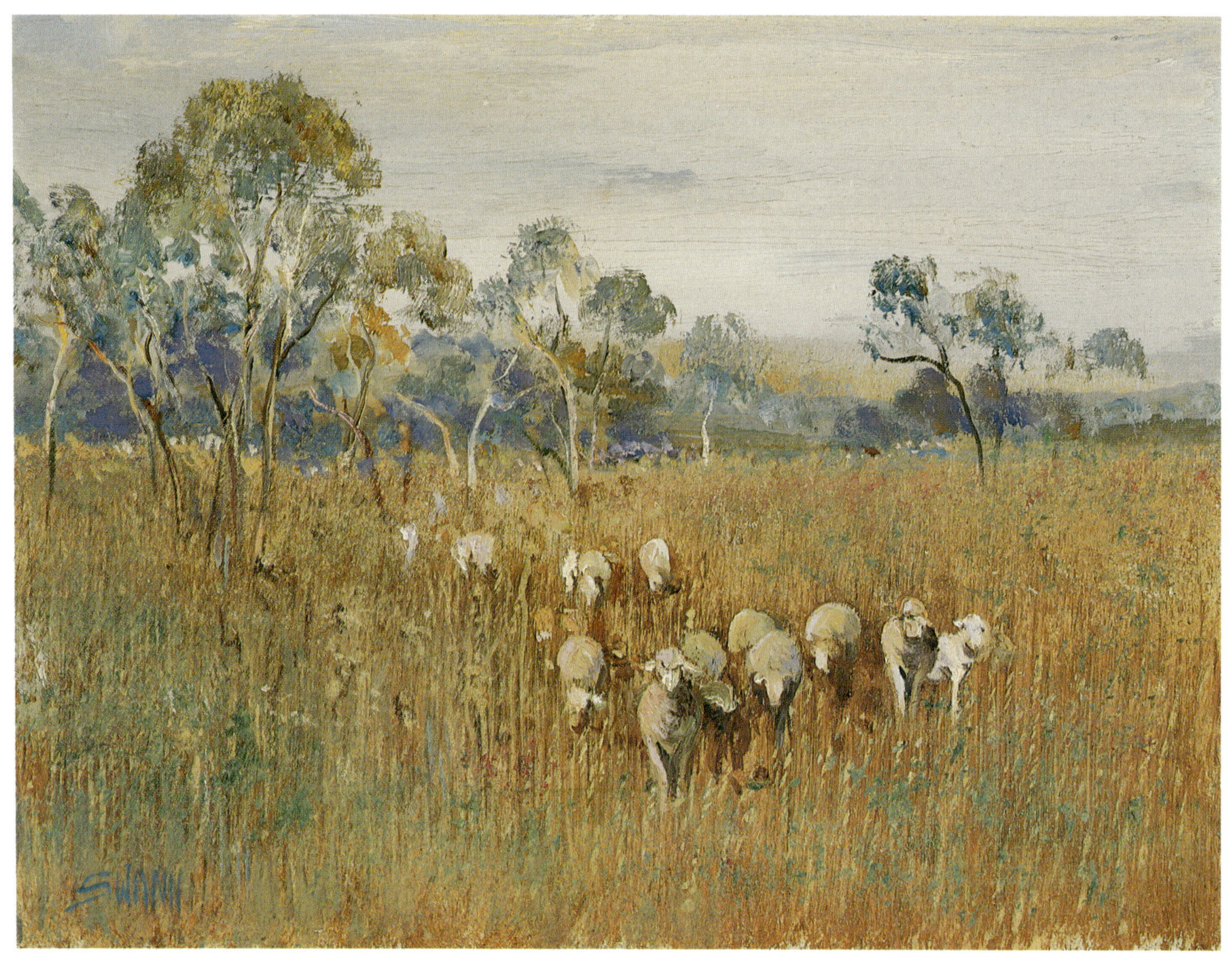

Hoggets

When they are about one year old, lambs lose two of their milk teeth, and two larger permanent teeth appear. They are then called 'two tooths' or 'hoggets'.

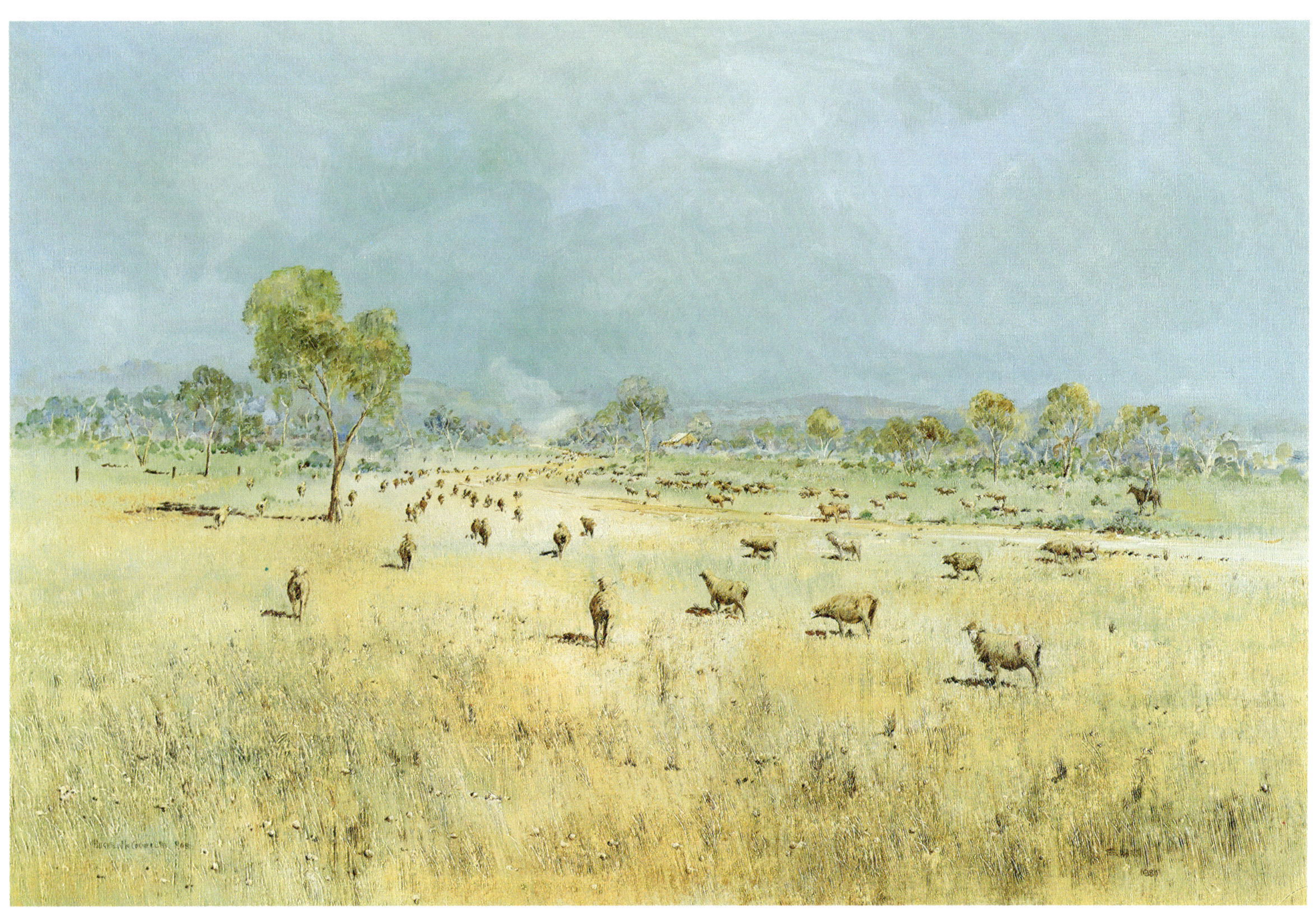

Hughie McConnell's mob

Hughie, veteran of World War I, was a blade shearer, drover and saleyard stockman. In my younger days at Mount Pleasant he taught me a great deal of stock sense.

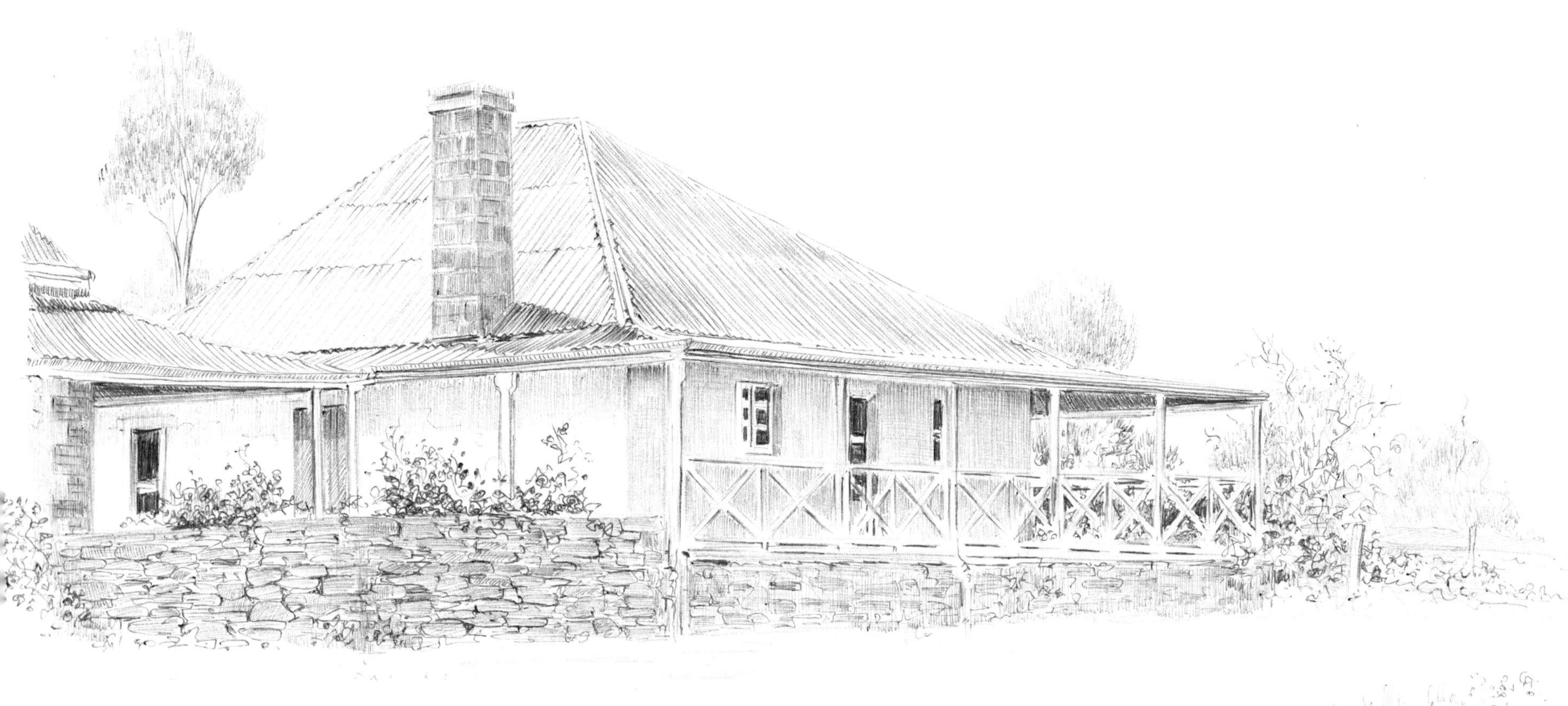

Mintaro cottage

*This was built in 1850 and is known as
Miller's House.*

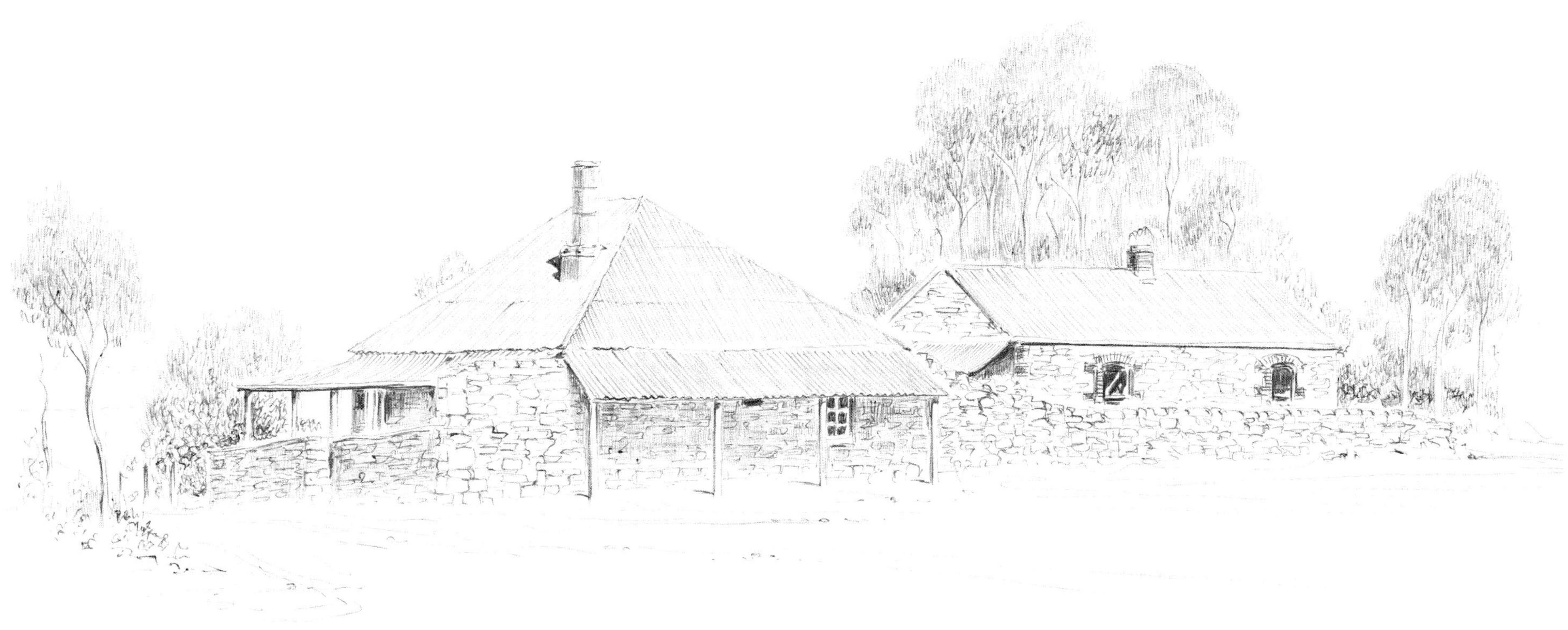

Mintaro cottage

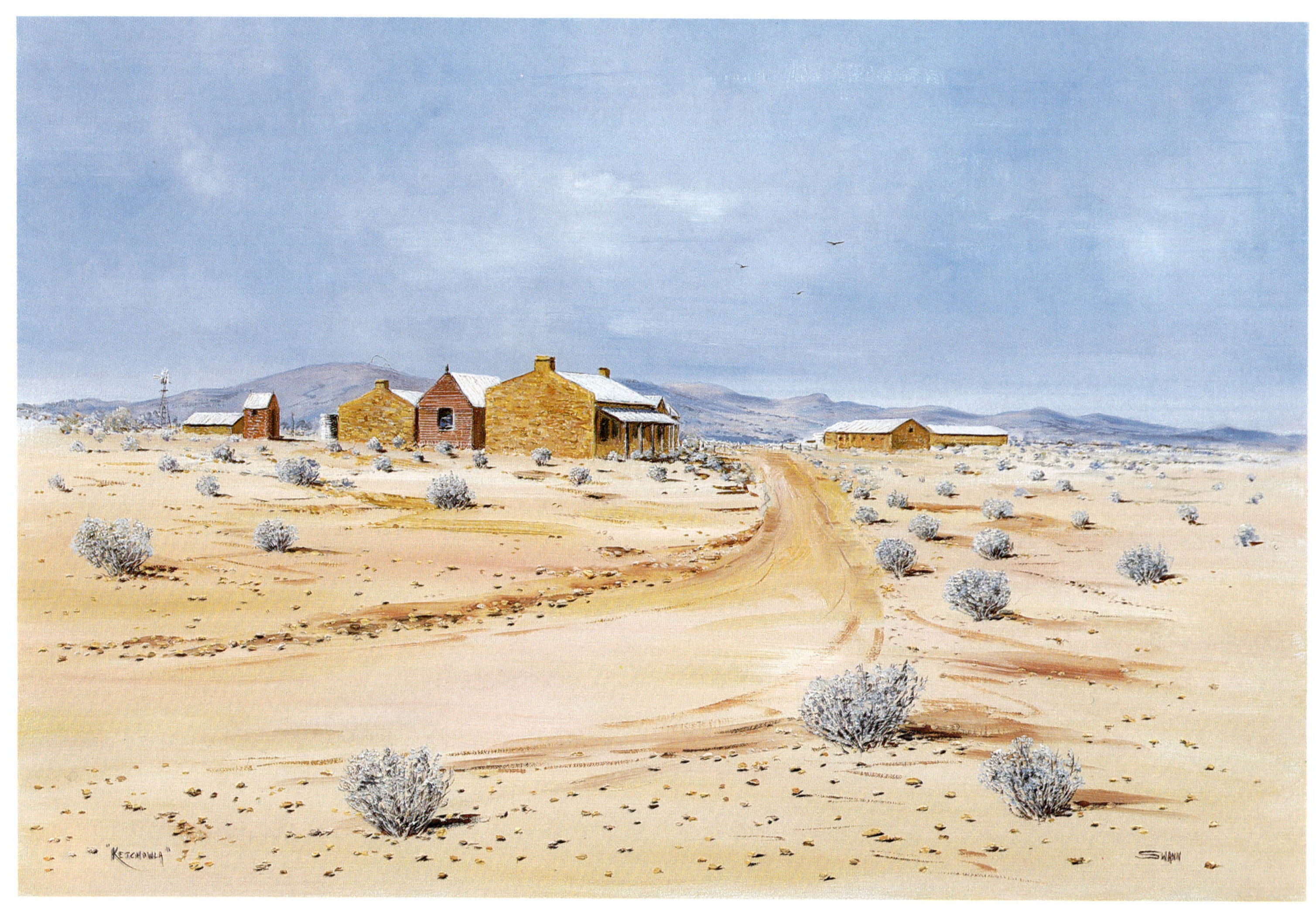

On Ketchowla Station

*Another view of the original stone building
built by the pioneering Dearlove family, whose
descendants still run this property.*

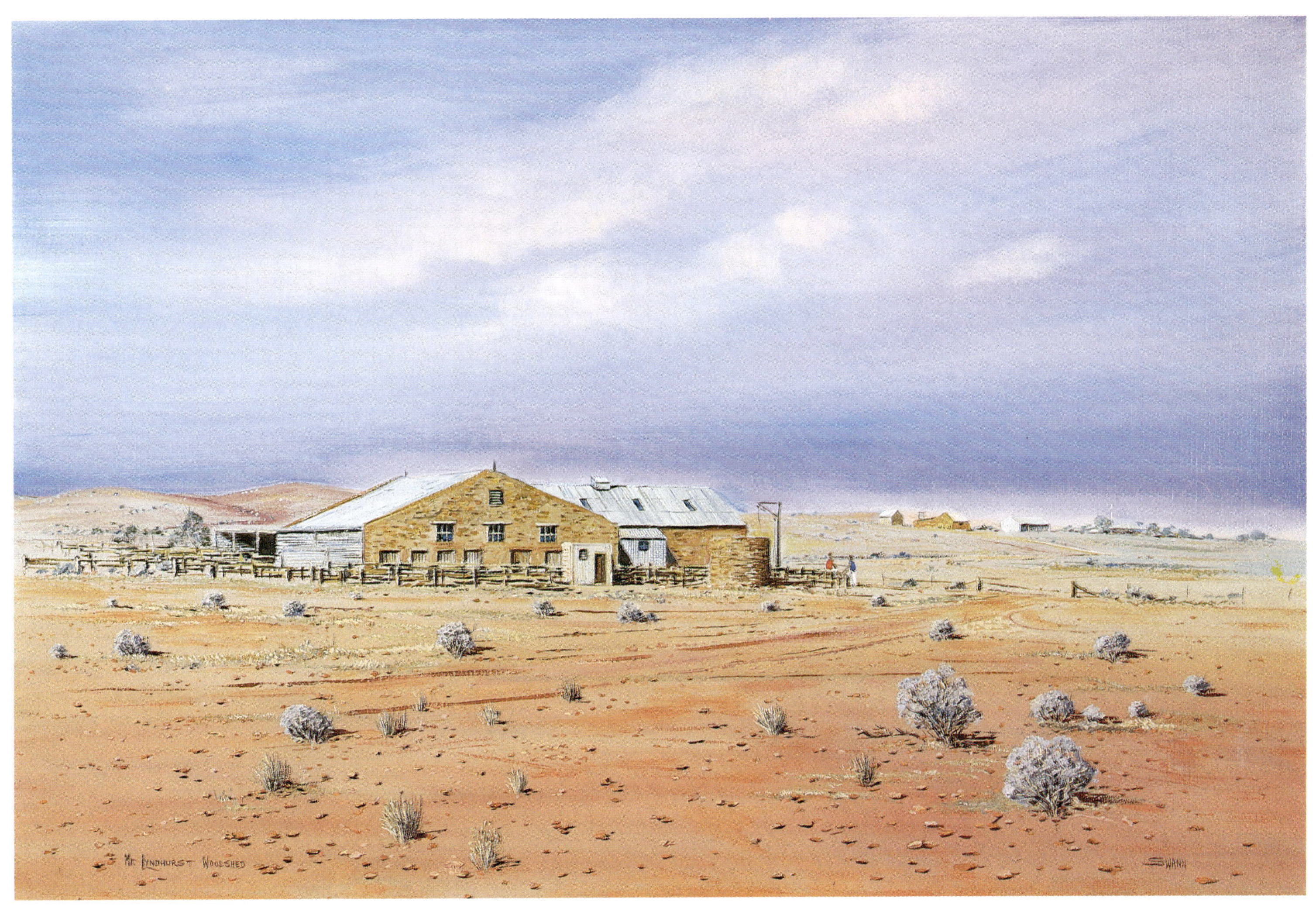

Mount Lyndhurst woolshed

The Station straddles the legendary Strzelecki Track. The area was taken up by Sir Thomas Elder, one of the founders of Elder Smith and Co. Ltd.

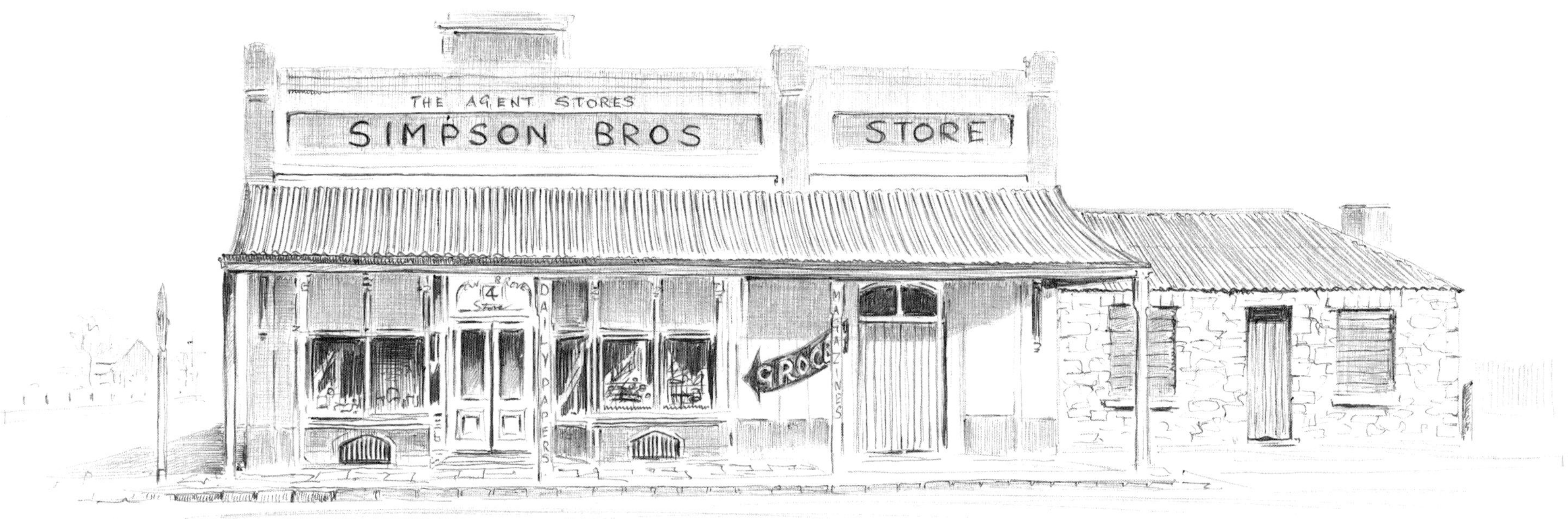

The store at Terowie

*Once this township was a busy railway
junction, but the new standard gauge line has
bypassed it and it is now battling to survive.*

64

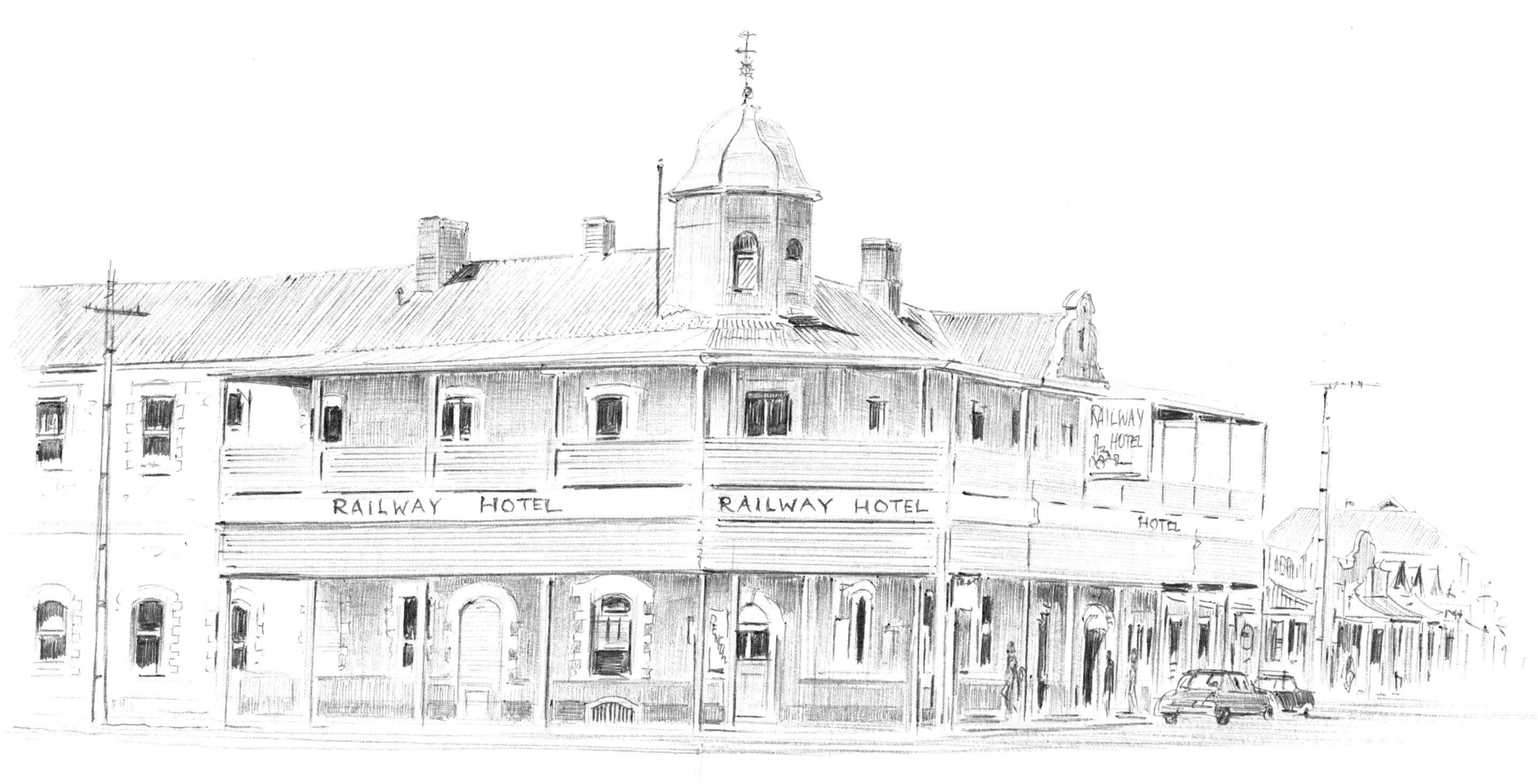

The Railway Hotel

Every country town has one! This is the one at Peterborough, a town which prospered mainly because of railway workshops and trans-shipping yards.

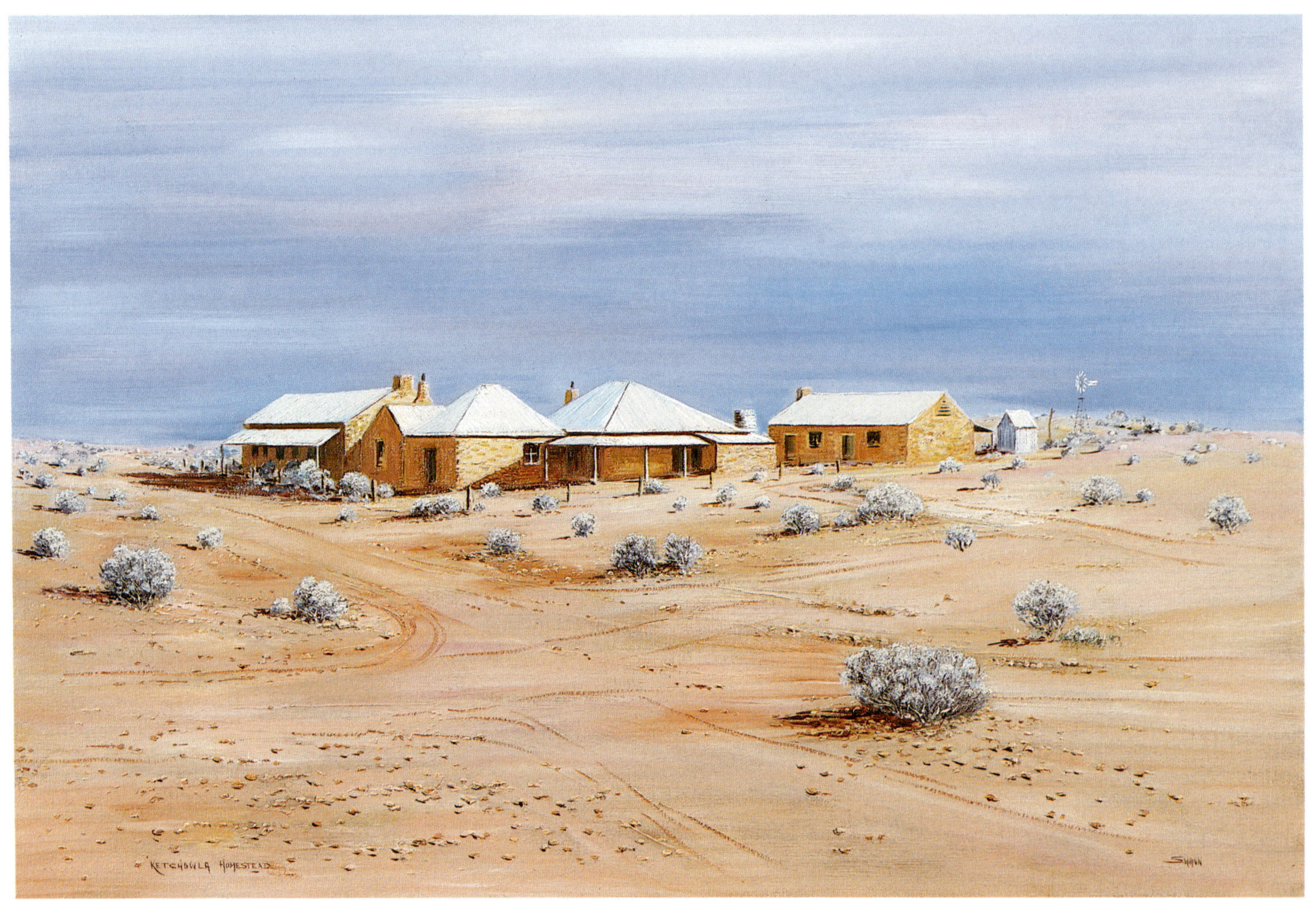

The old homestead at Ketchowla

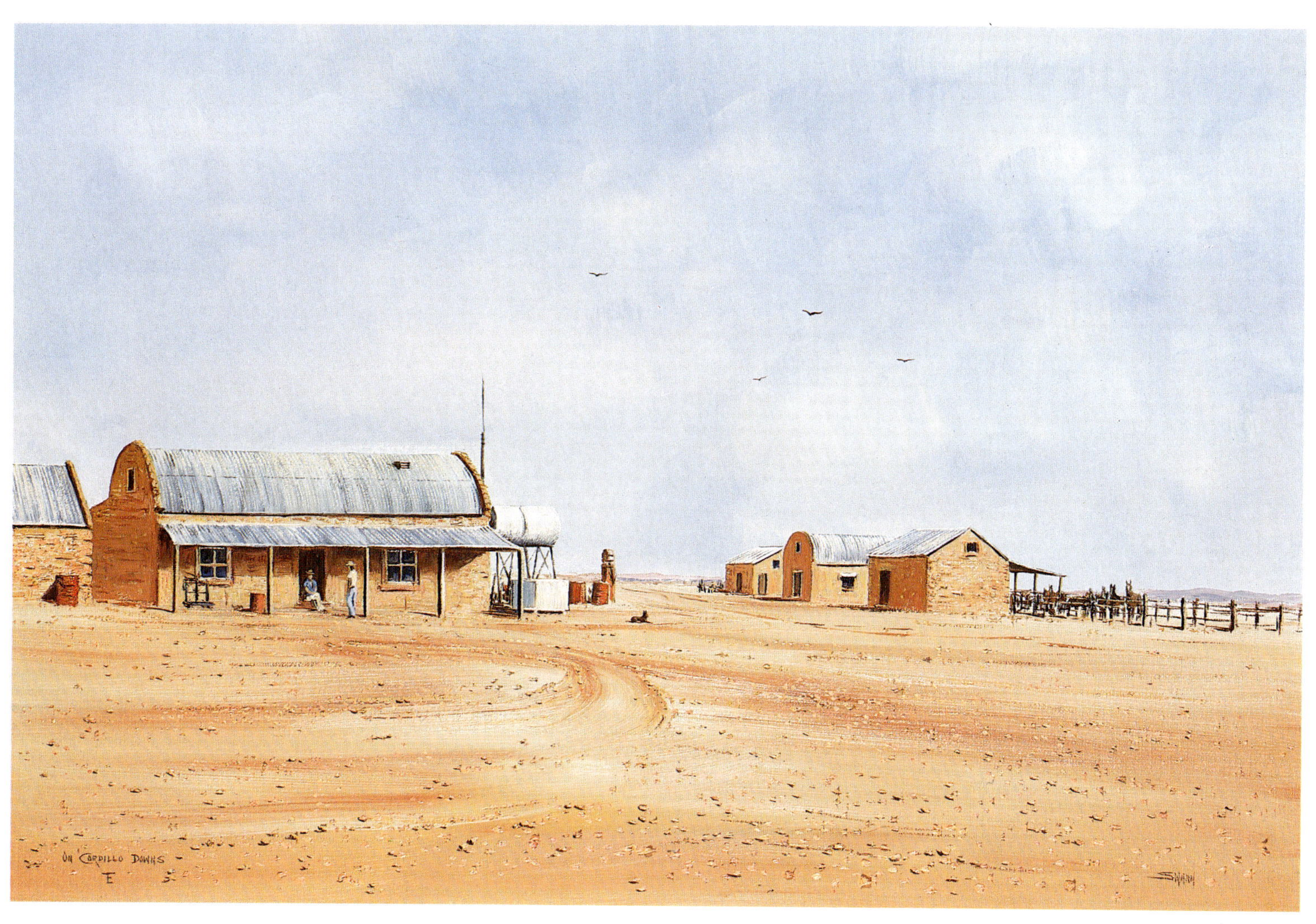

On Cordillo Downs Station in the
remote north-east

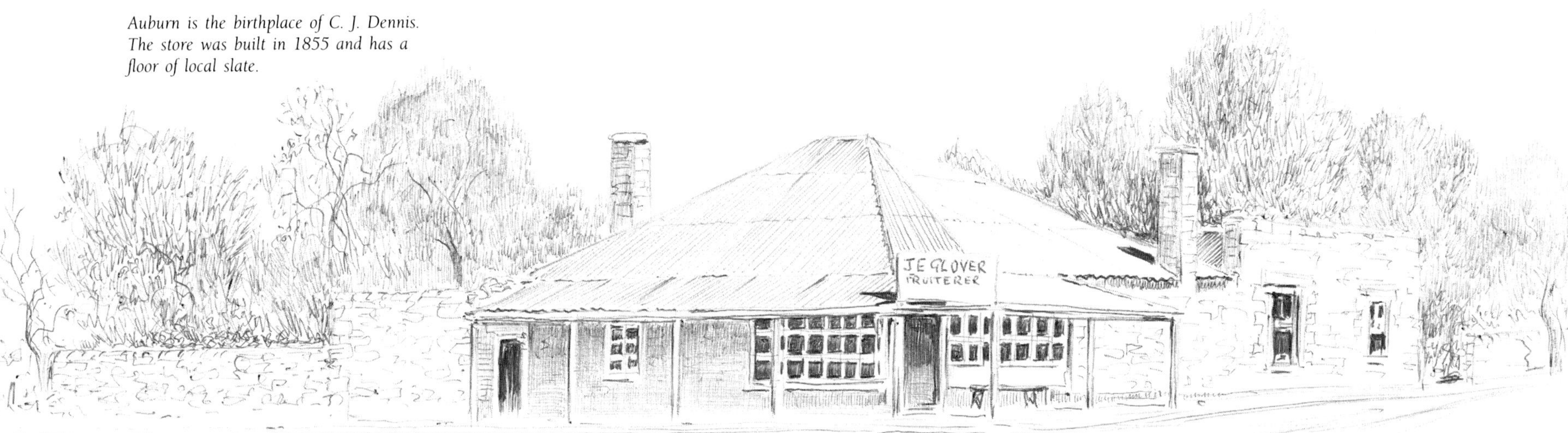

At Auburn in the Mid North

Auburn is the birthplace of C. J. Dennis. The store was built in 1855 and has a floor of local slate.

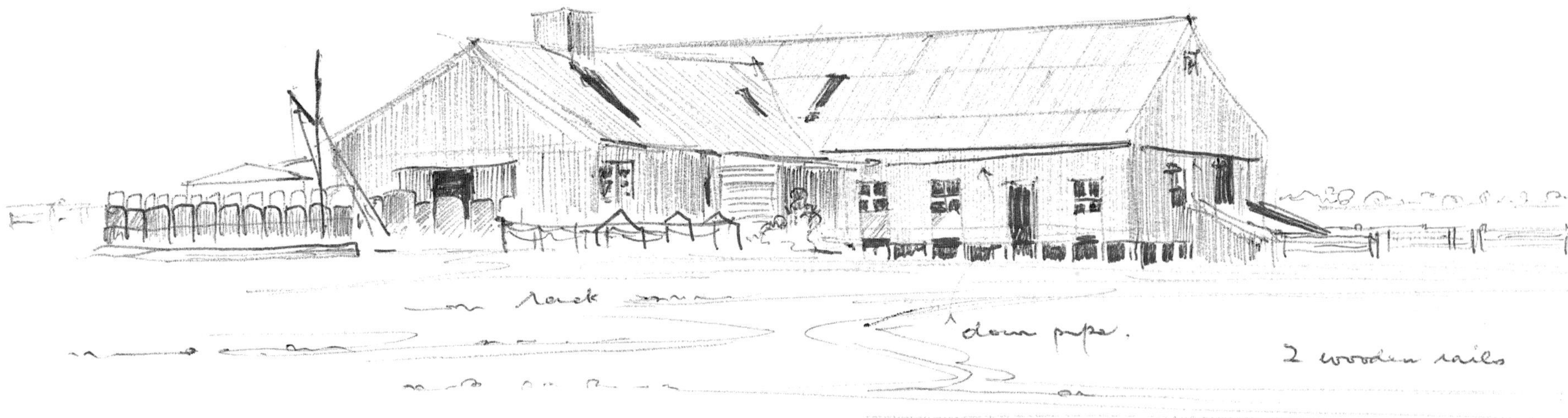

Mount Eba woolshed, Kingoonya

Stockport railway station

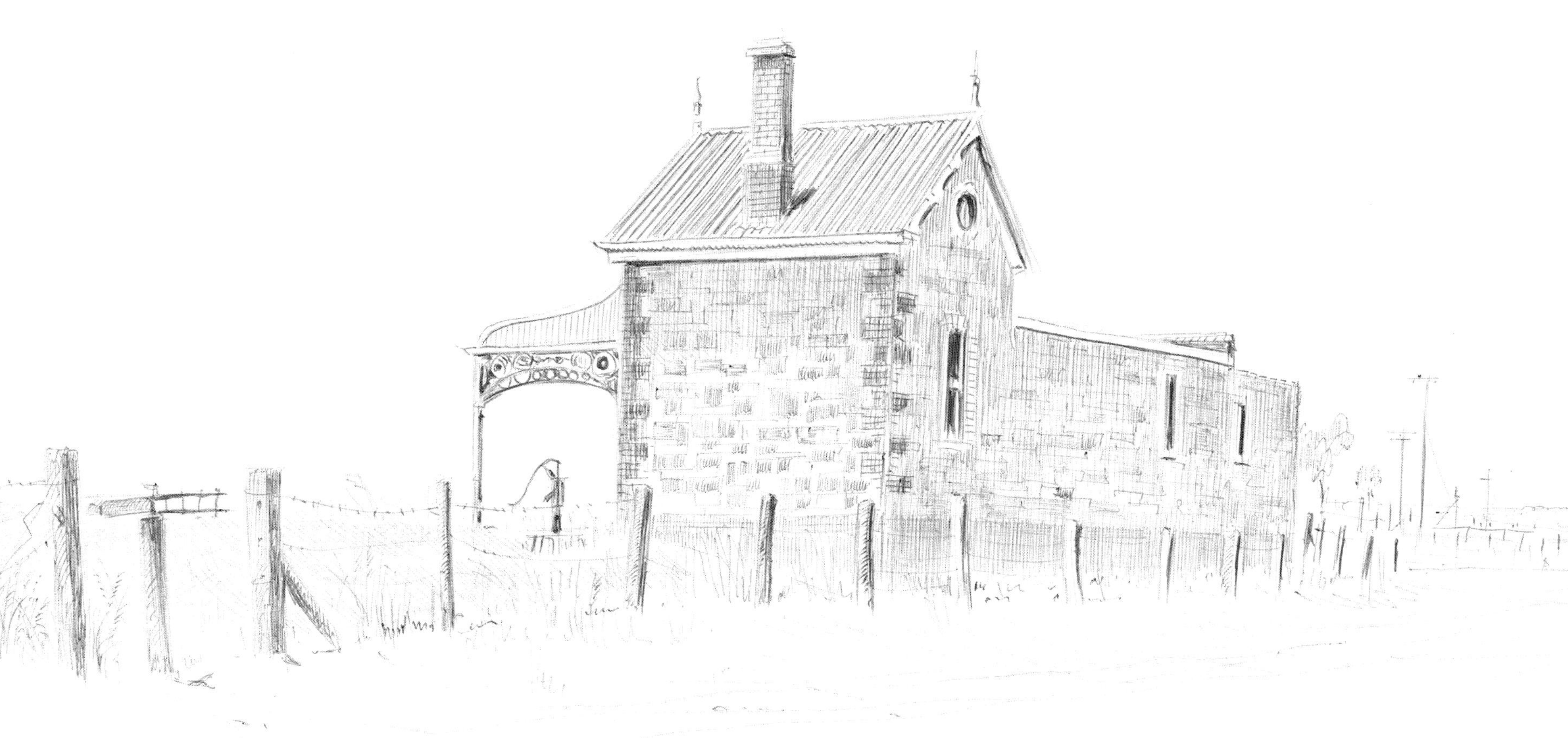

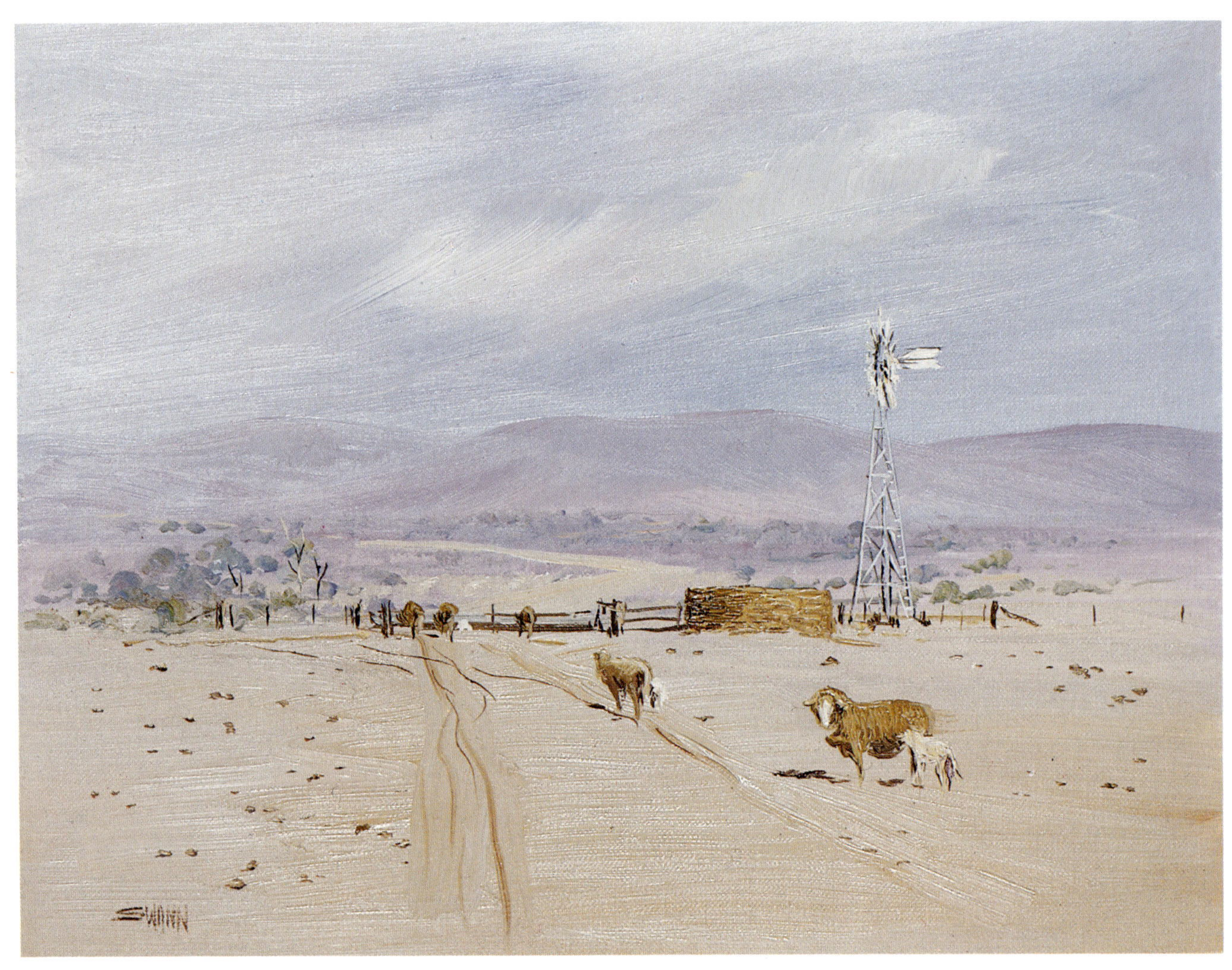

Ewes and lambs watering, Gawler
Ranges

70

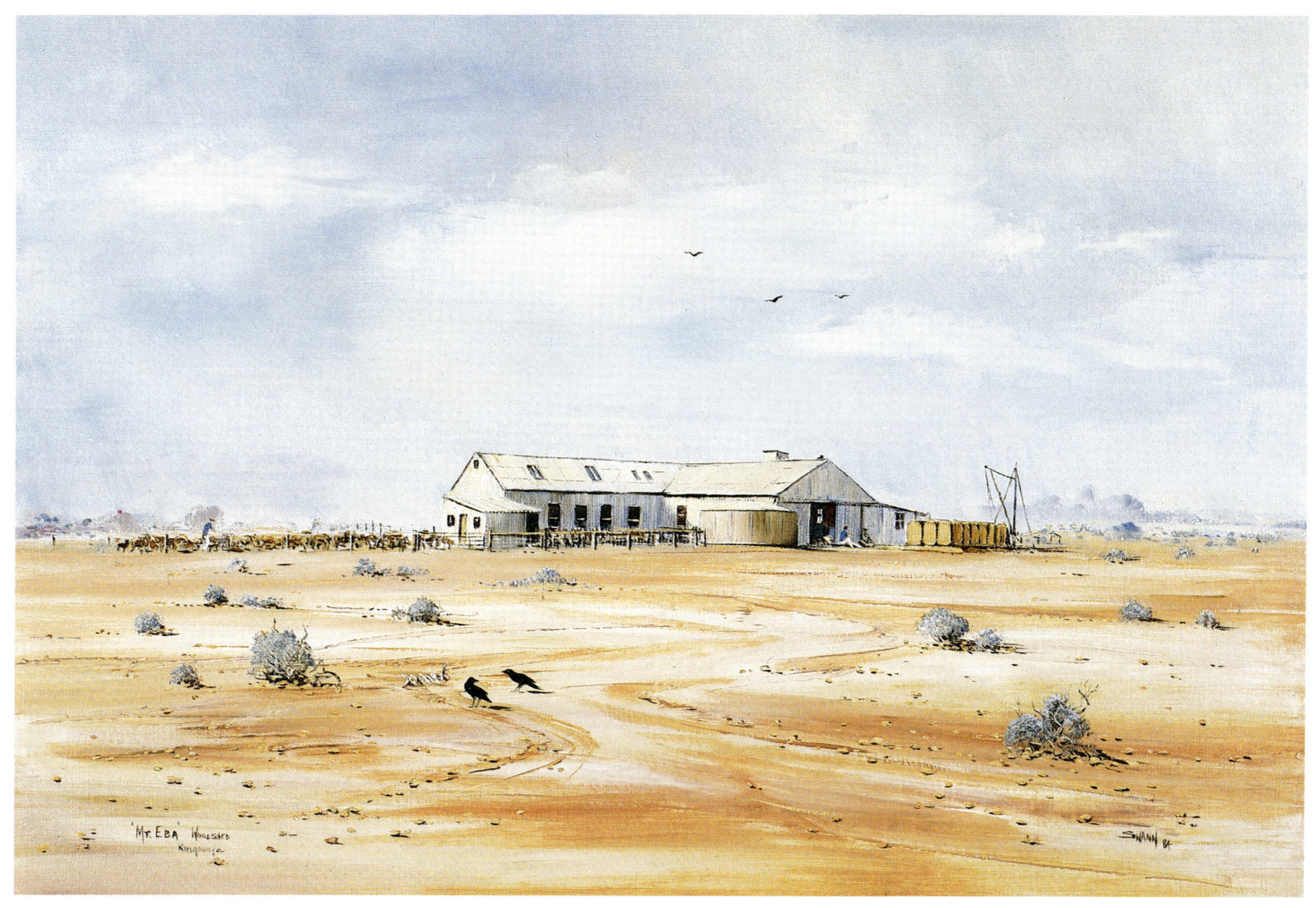

Mount Eba woolshed

This run is in the isolated and dry north-west of the State. When I painted the scene, shearing was in progress. A team of six shearers had been hired to shear 18,000 sheep.

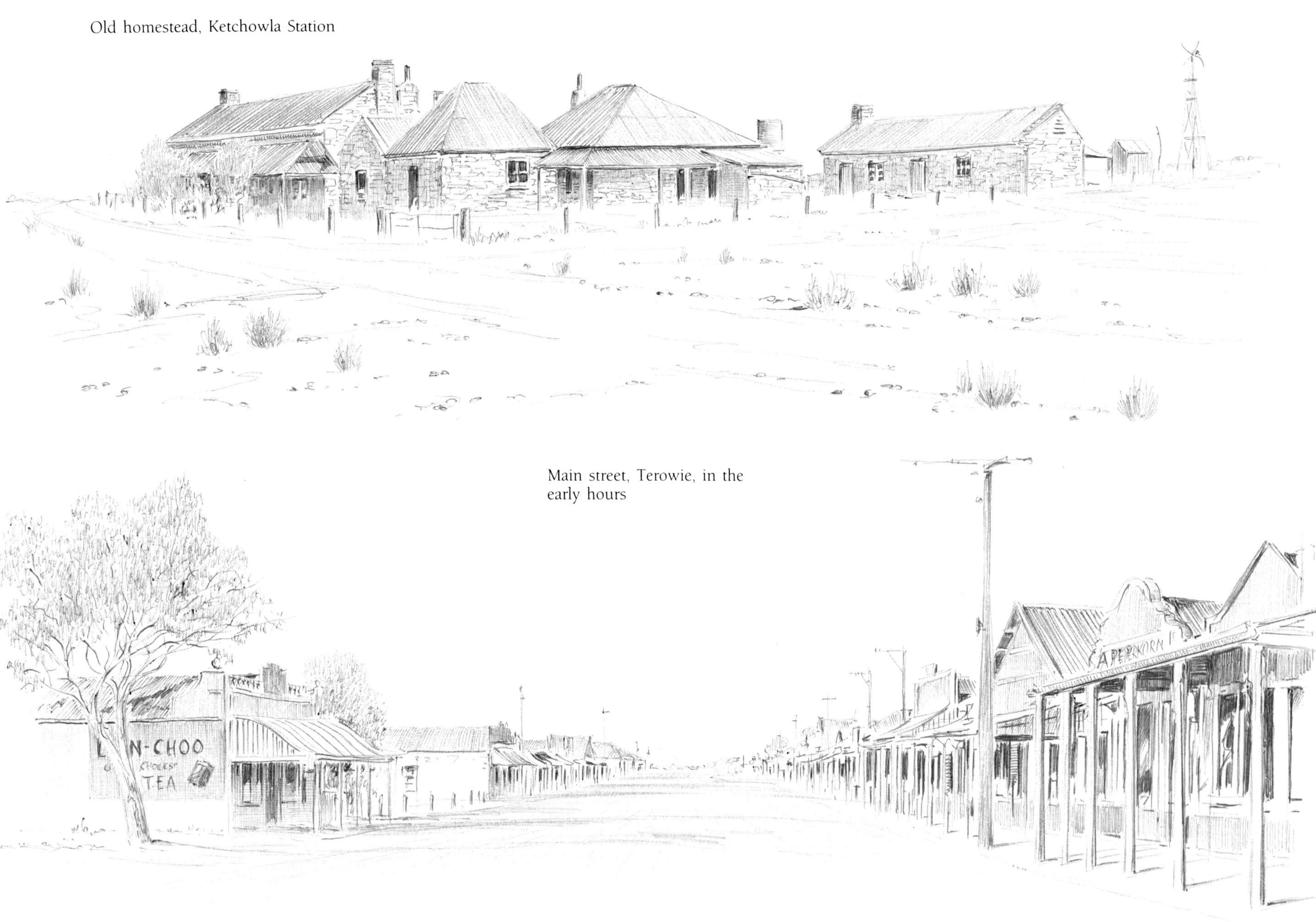

Old homestead, Ketchowla Station

Main street, Terowie, in the
early hours

72

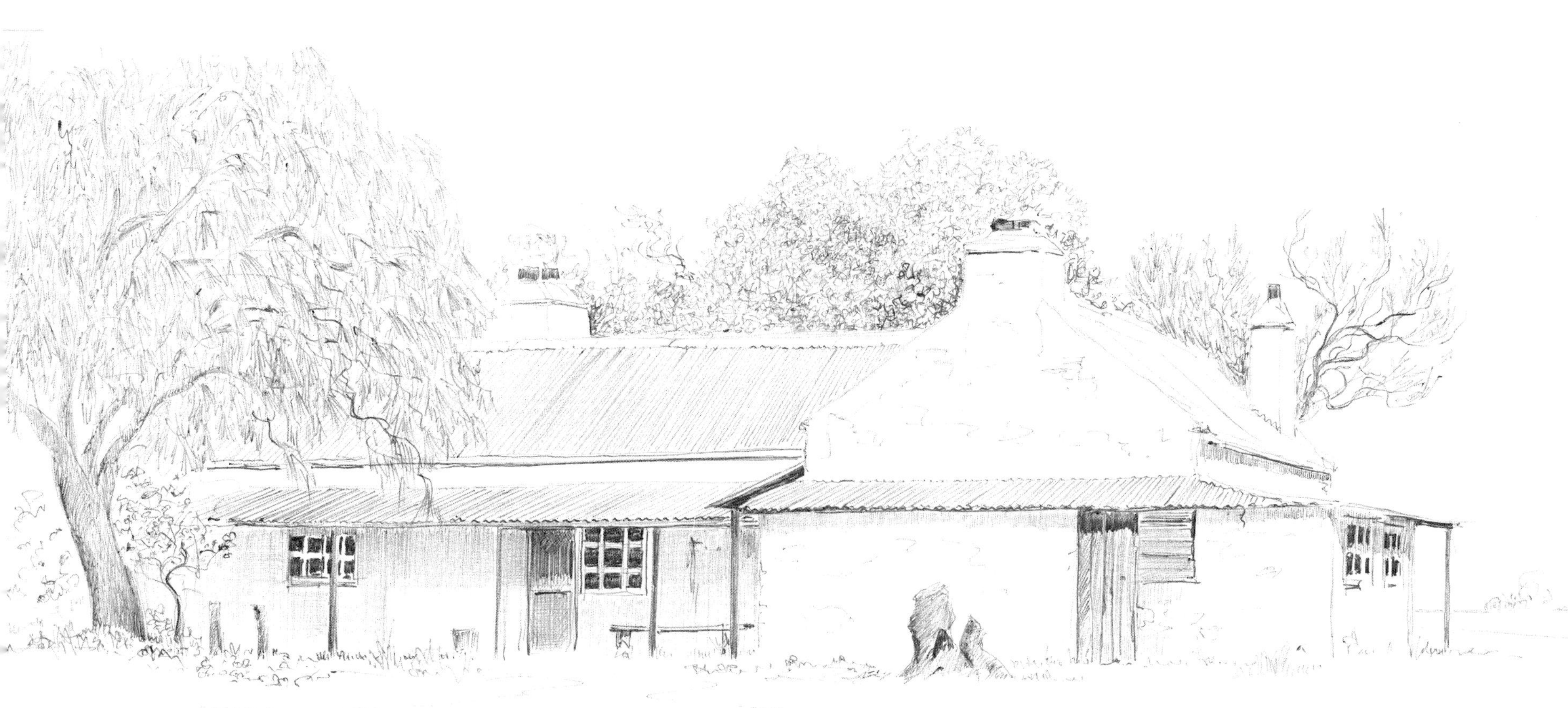

Denings' Farm, Robe

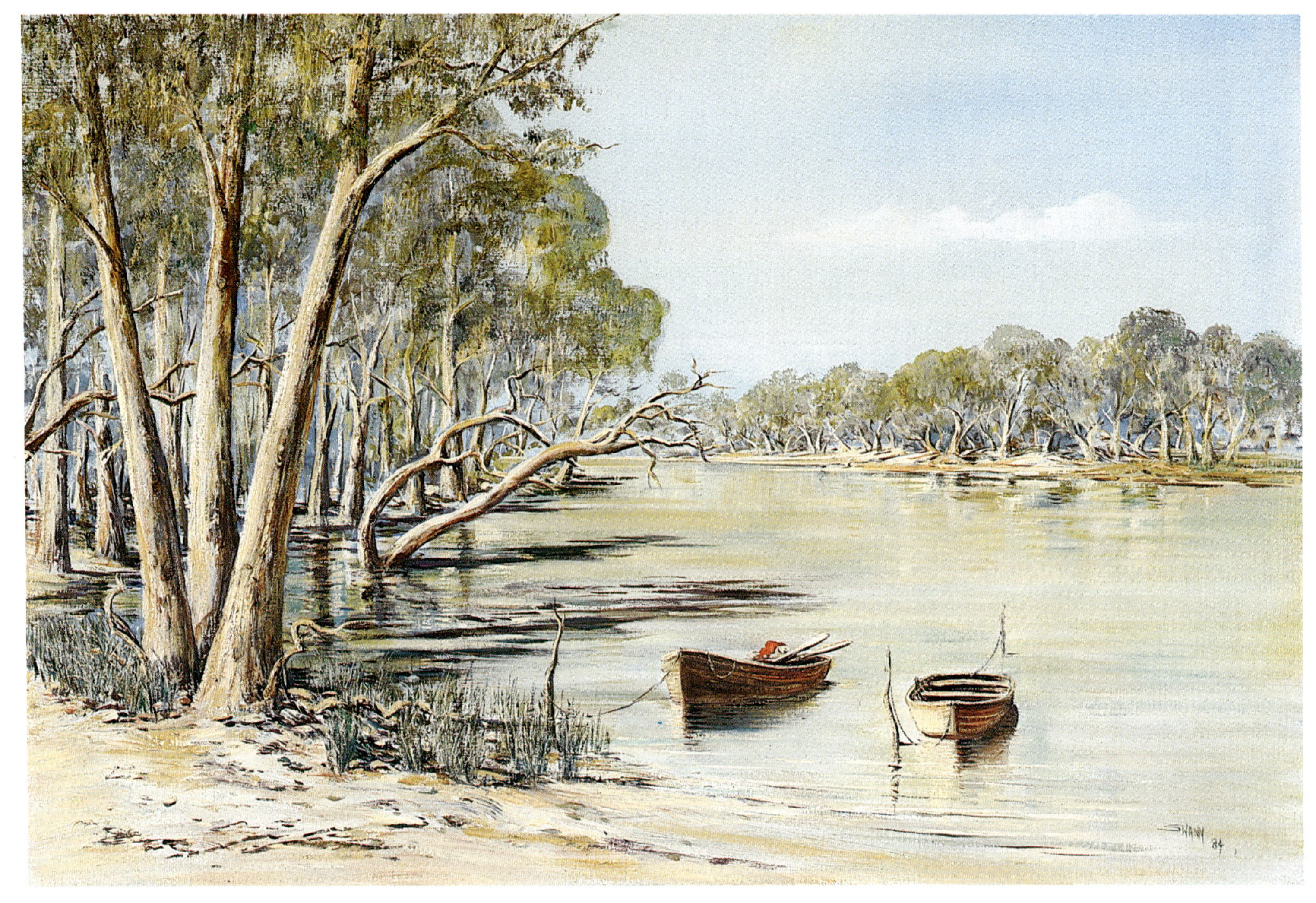

Meander, River Murray

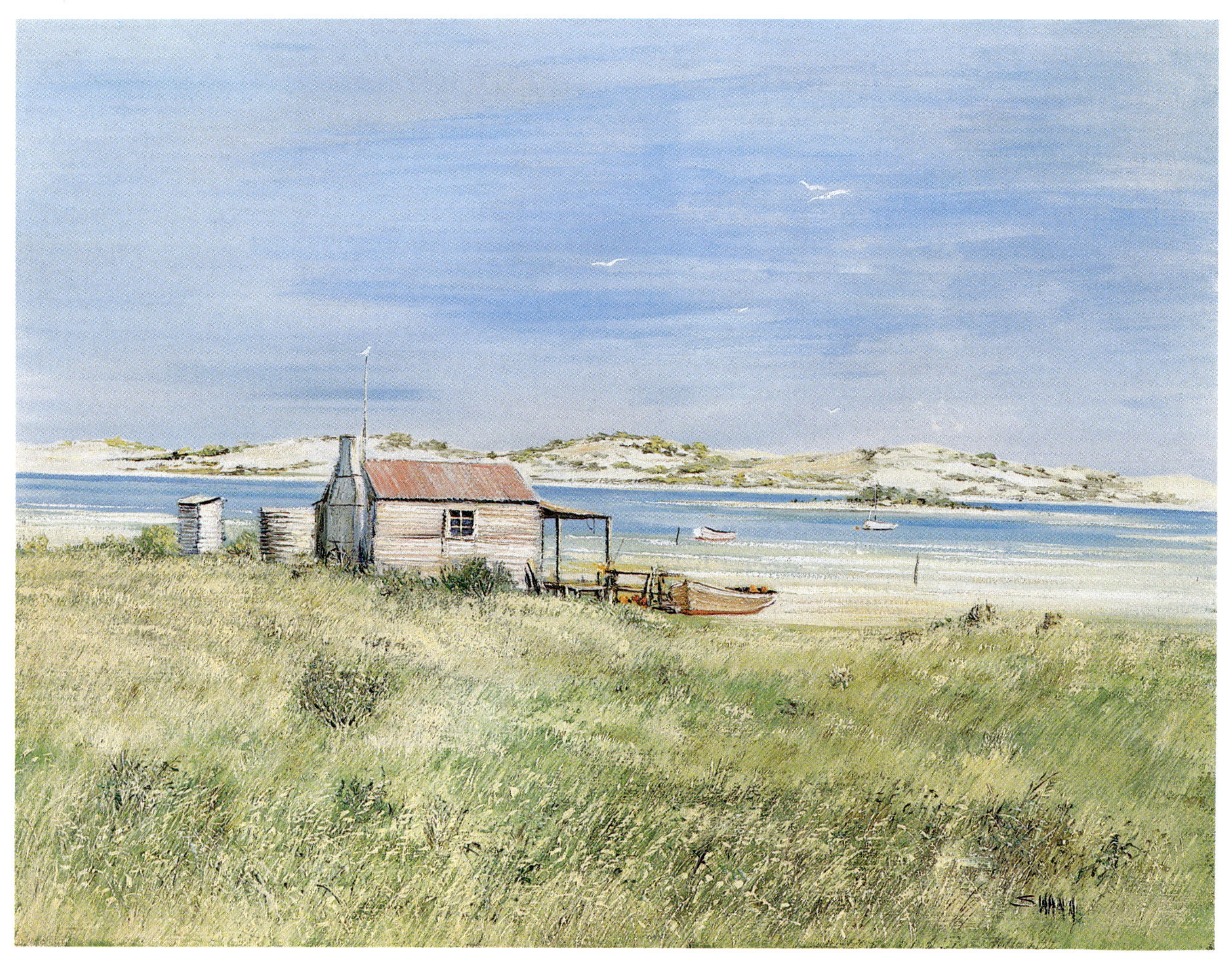

Fisherman's shack, Coorong

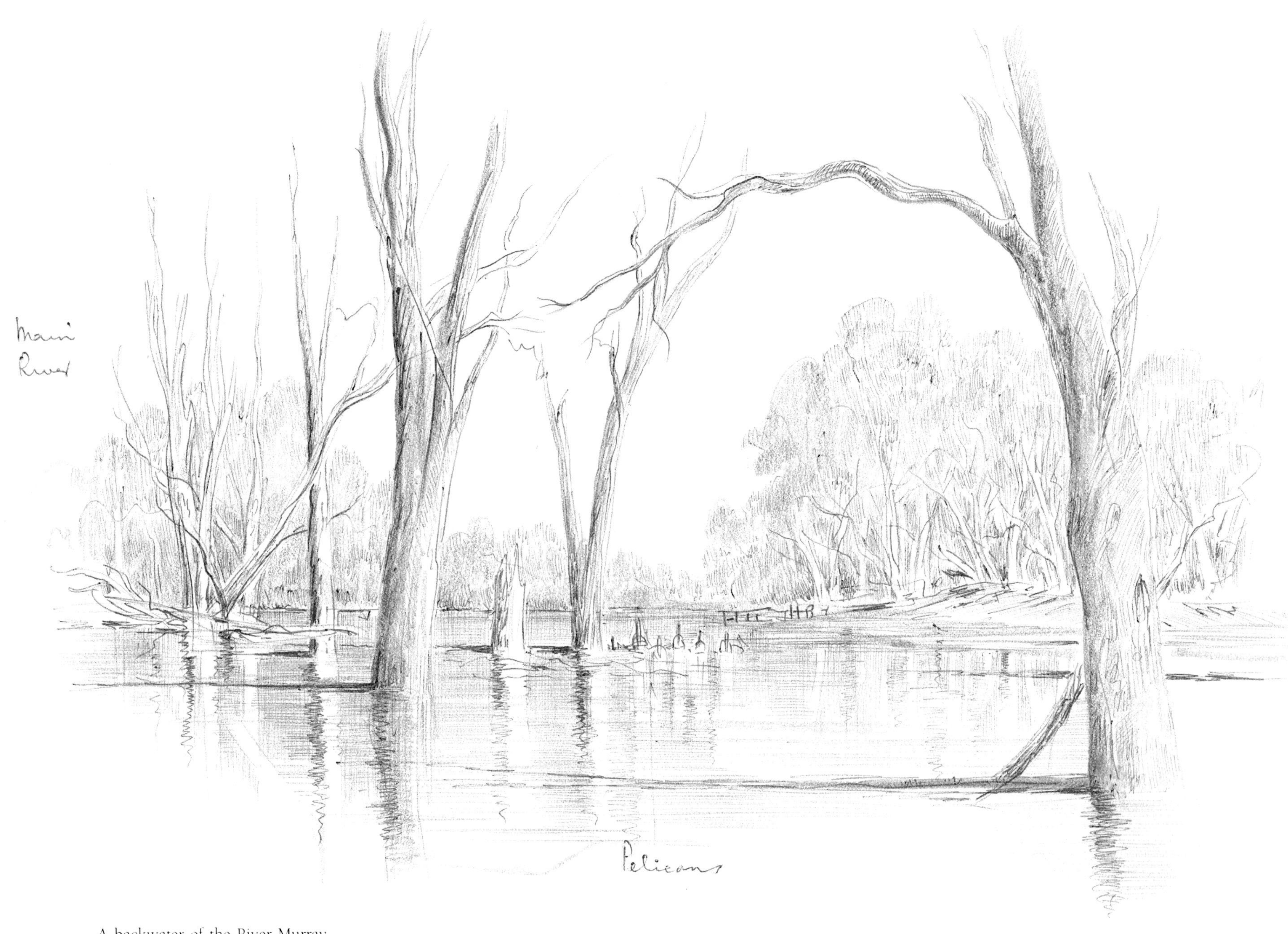

A backwater of the River Murray

76

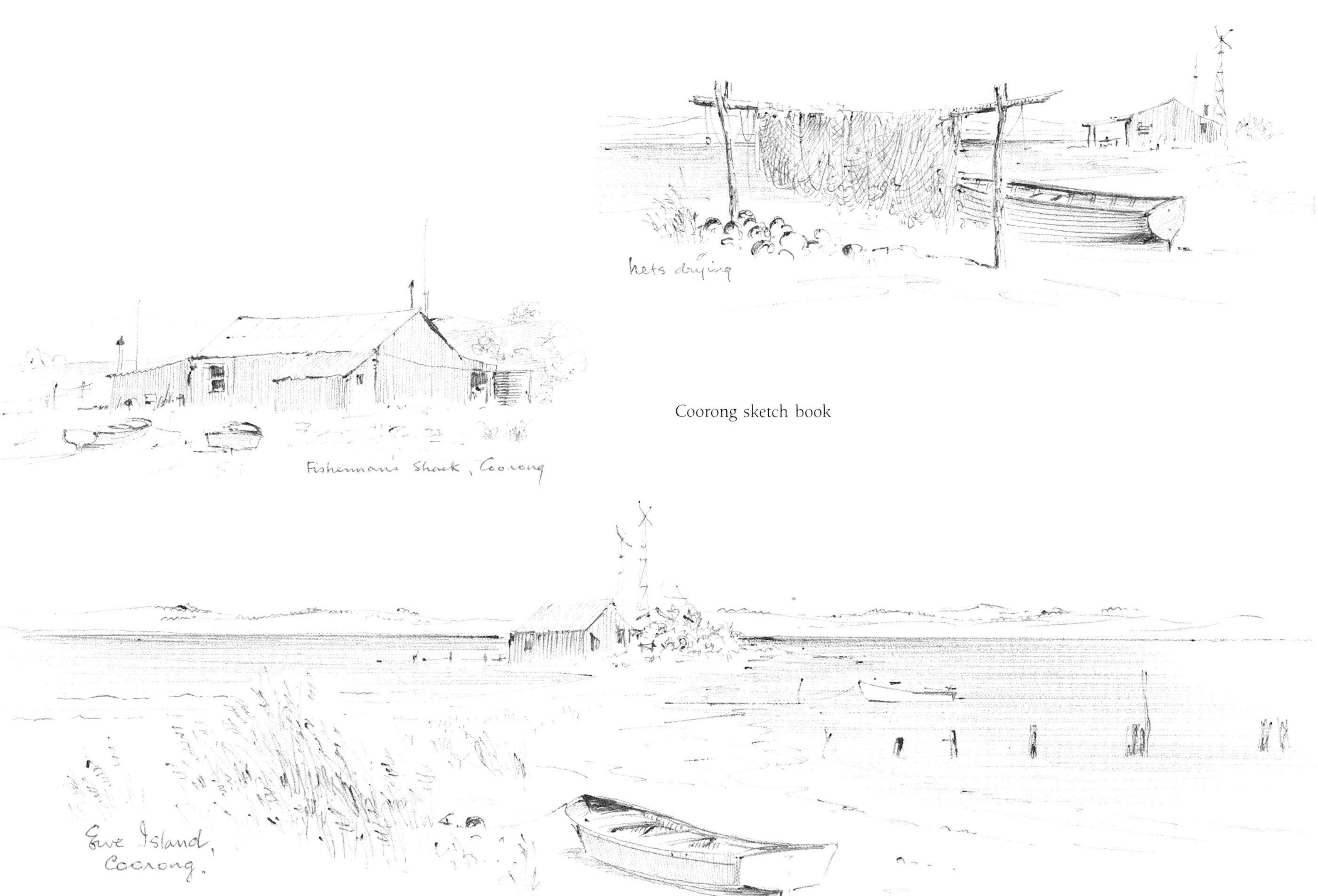

Coorong sketch book

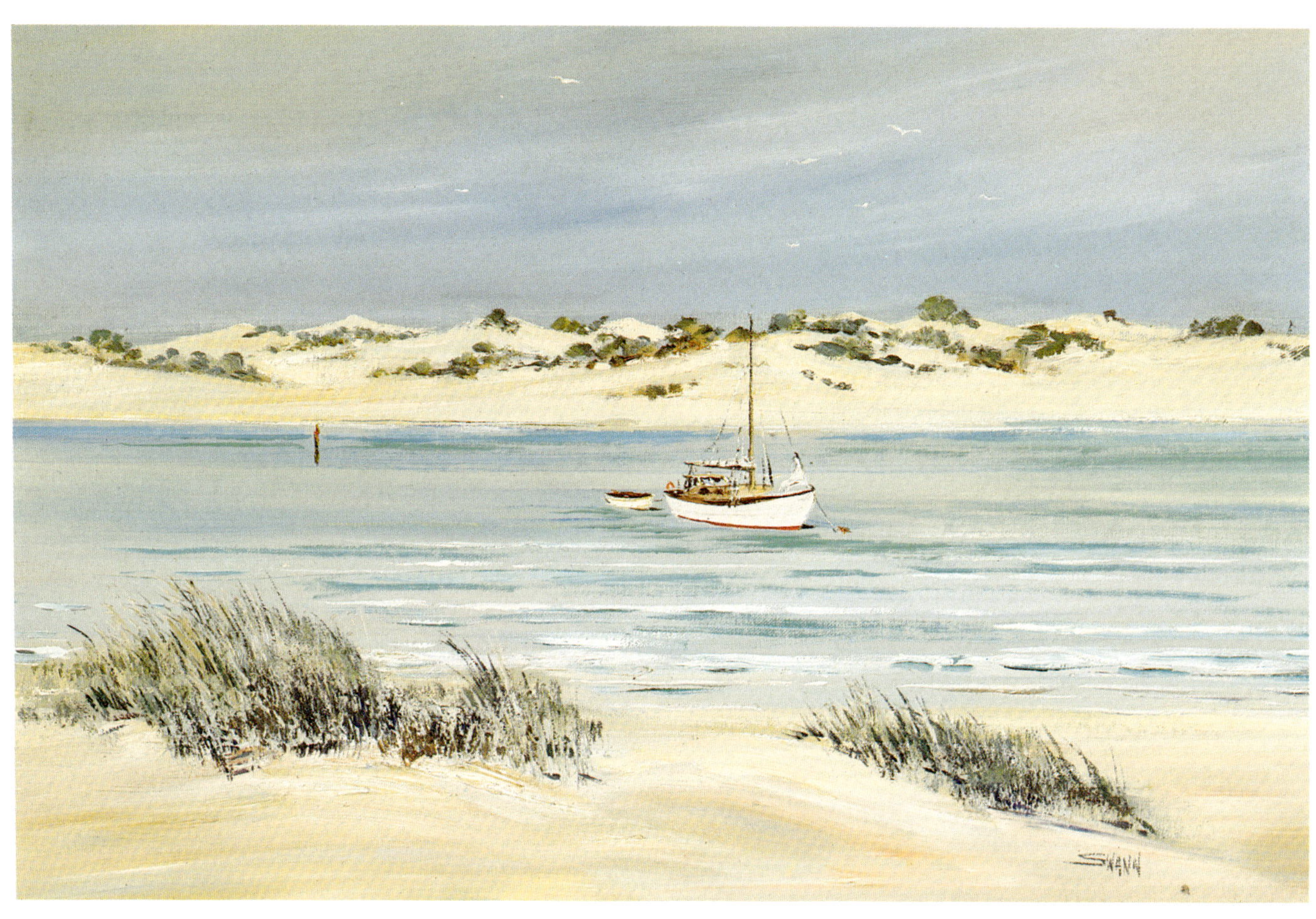

The Coorong

Kurangh—the Neck—was the aboriginal name
for the great lagoon stretching nearly 150
kilometres inside the coastal dunes from the
River Murray mouth to Lacepede Bay.

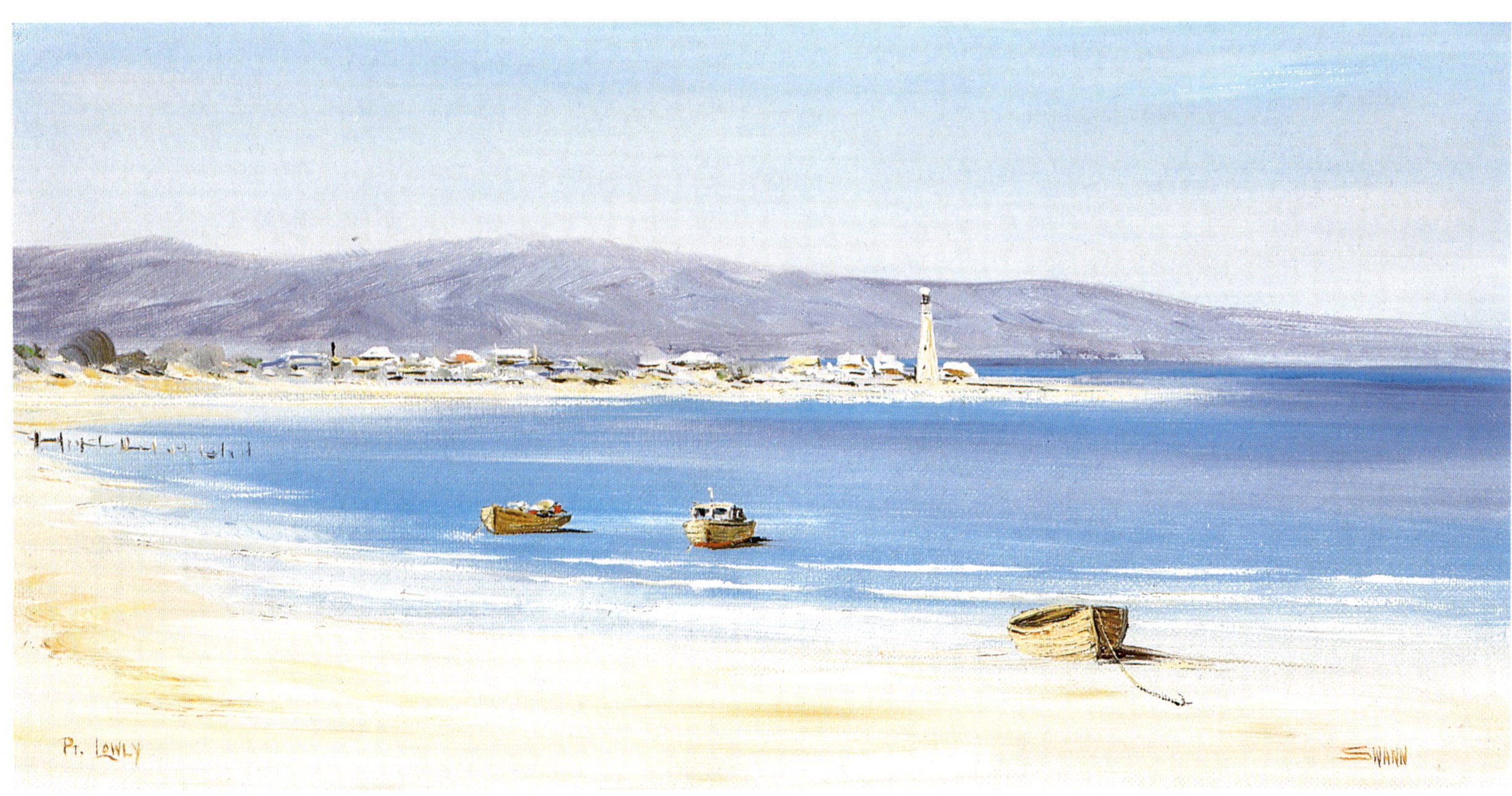

Point Lowly, near Whyalla

Golden sand, cobalt and turquoise shoal waters sparkle under the strong clear sky. The far distant peaks of the Flinders Ranges shimmer in the heat. This unspoilt scene is within two kilometres of Port Bonython, the 300 million dollar hydro carbons liquid terminal, which started operations in 1984.

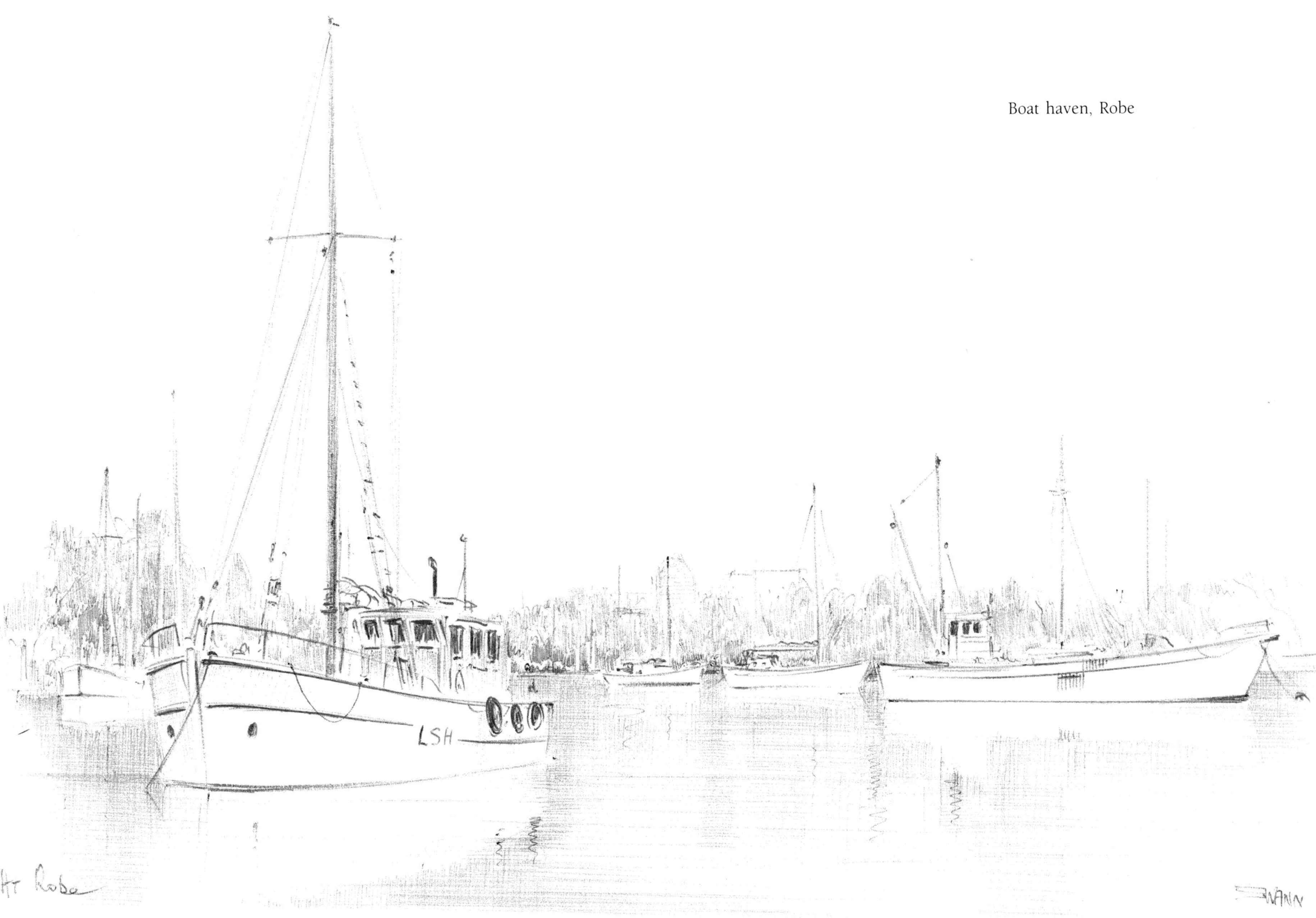

Boat haven, Robe

Boat haven, Robe

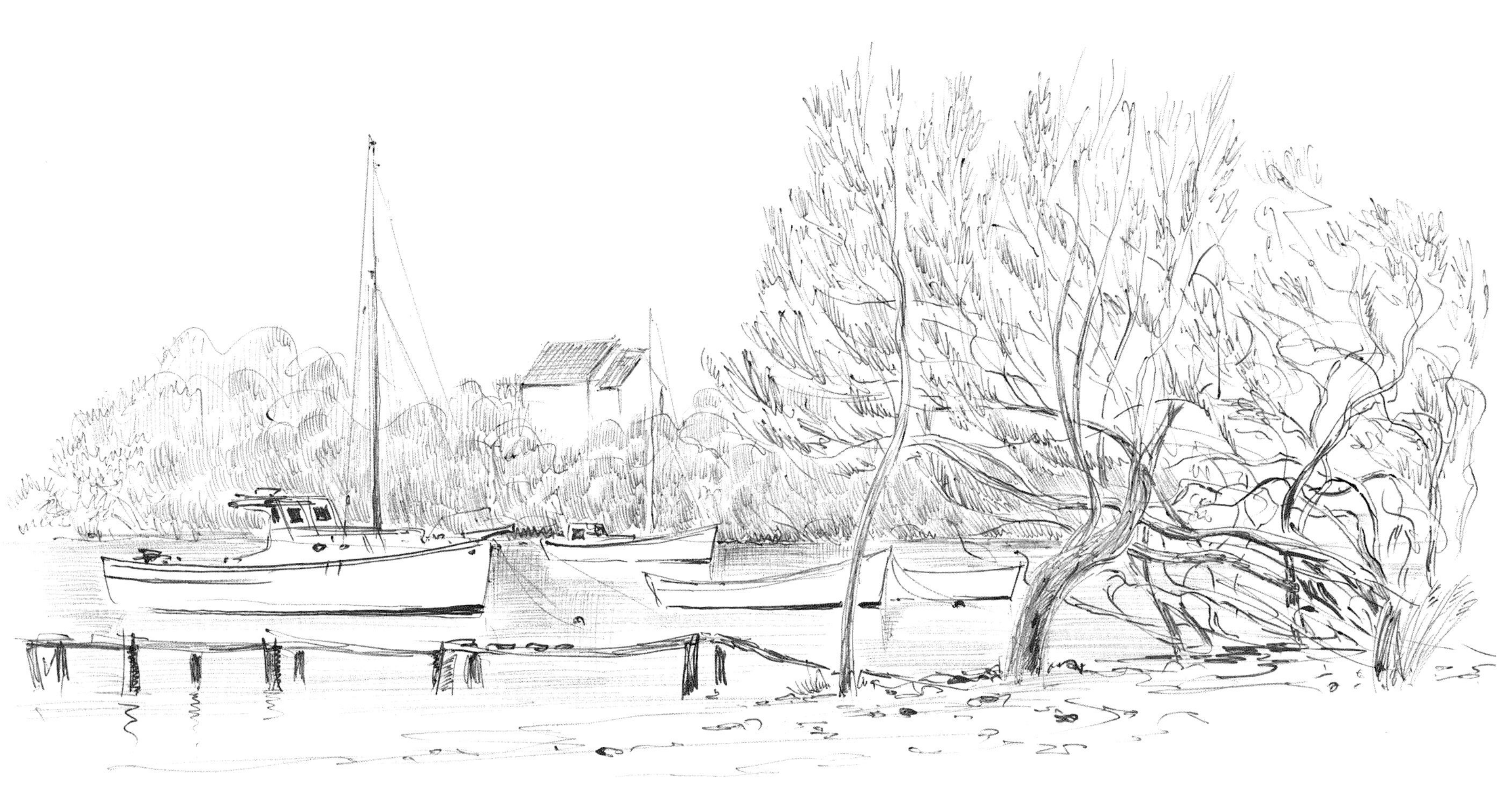

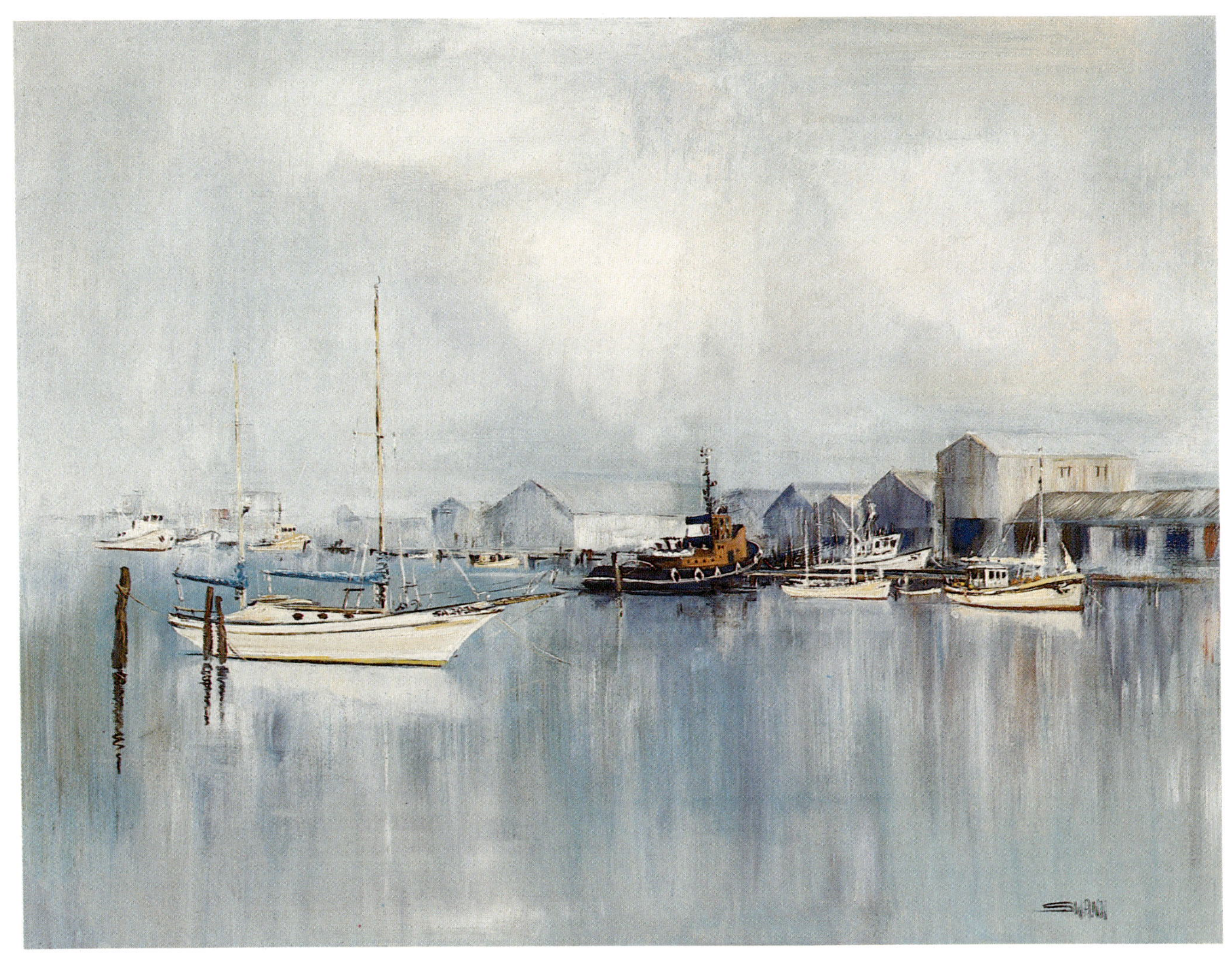

Beauty and the Beast

The gracious ketch Sari *is moored in the Port River with the sturdy little tugboat* Warrondi *in the background.*

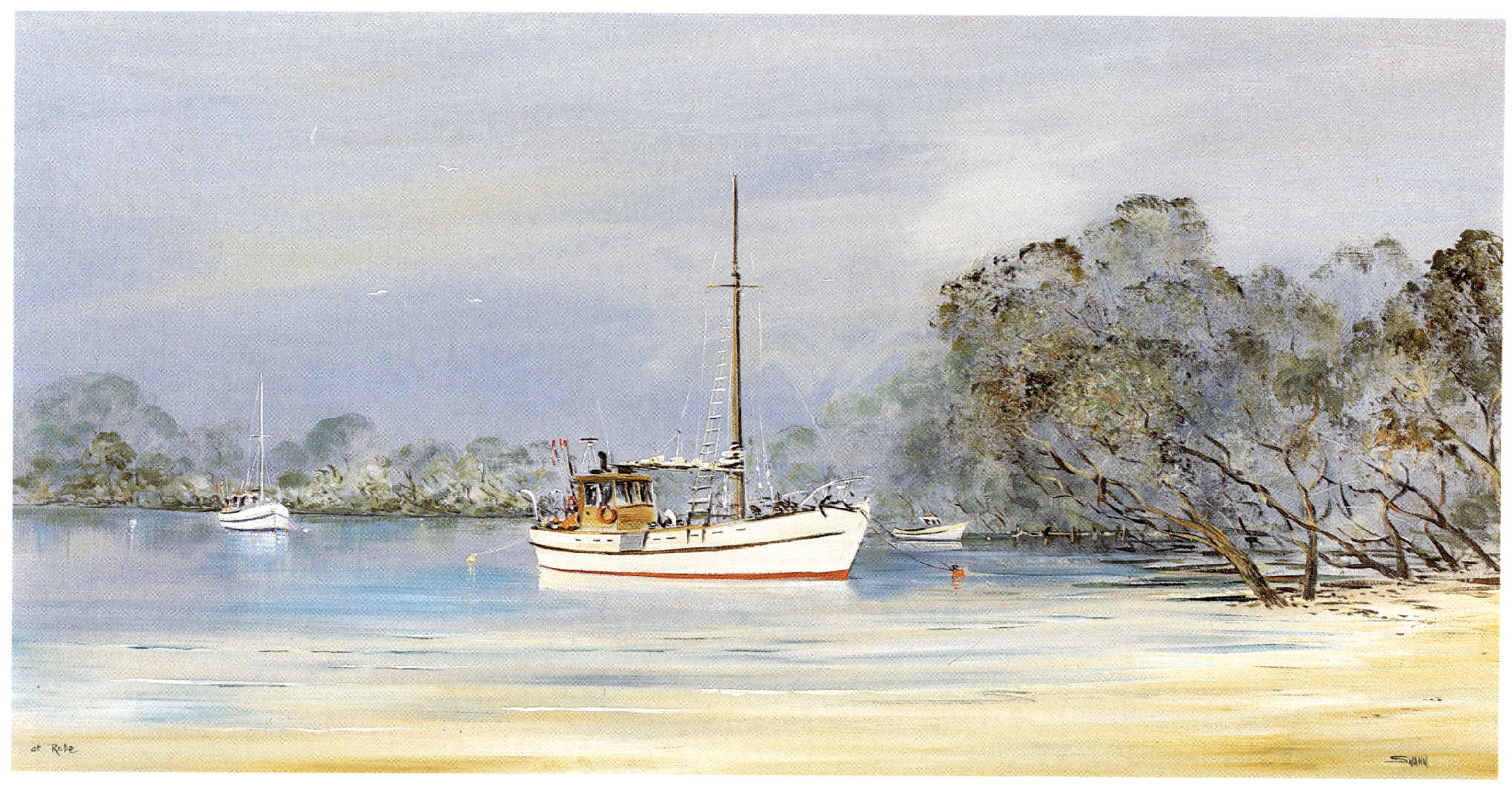

Robe

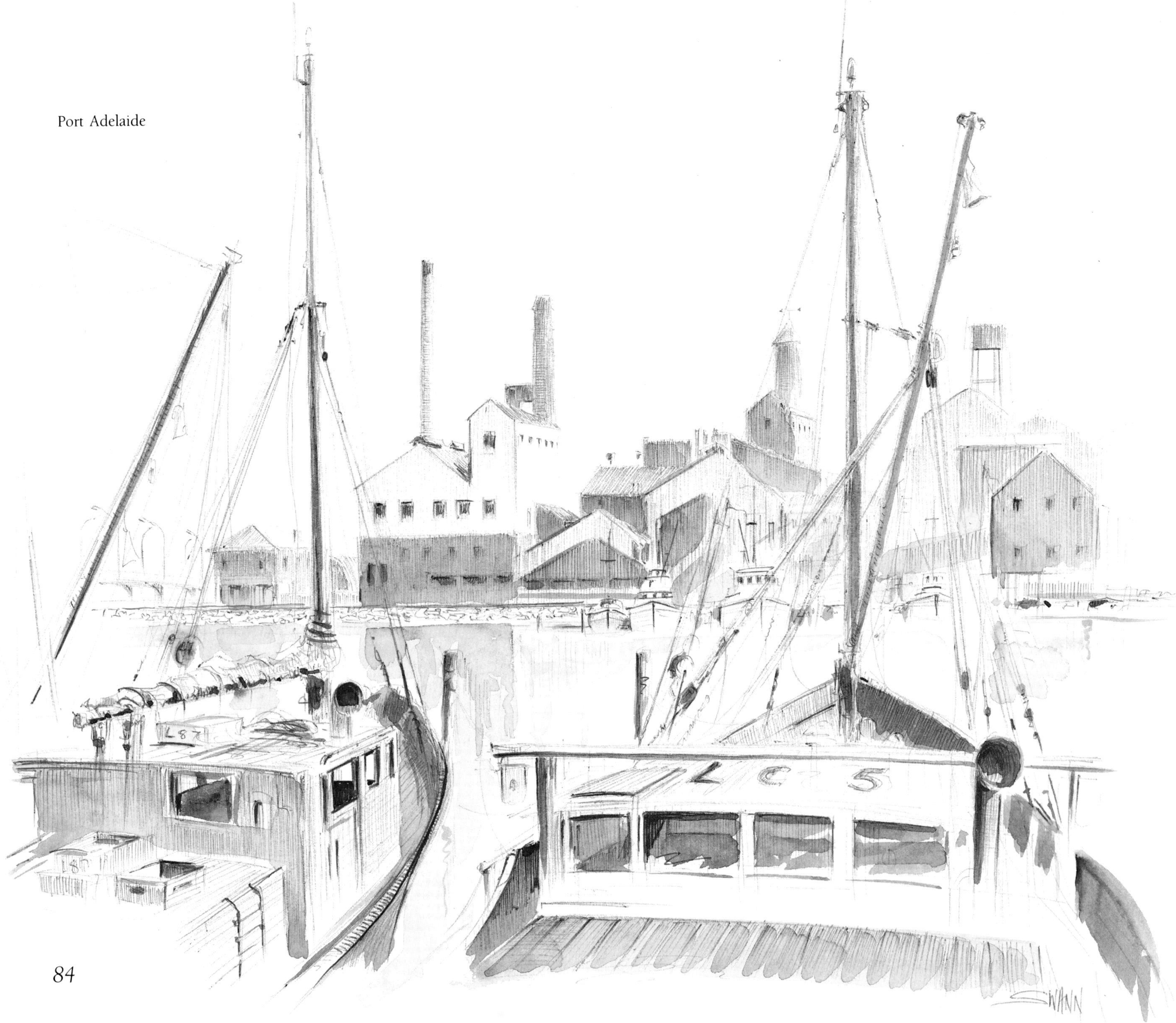
Port Adelaide

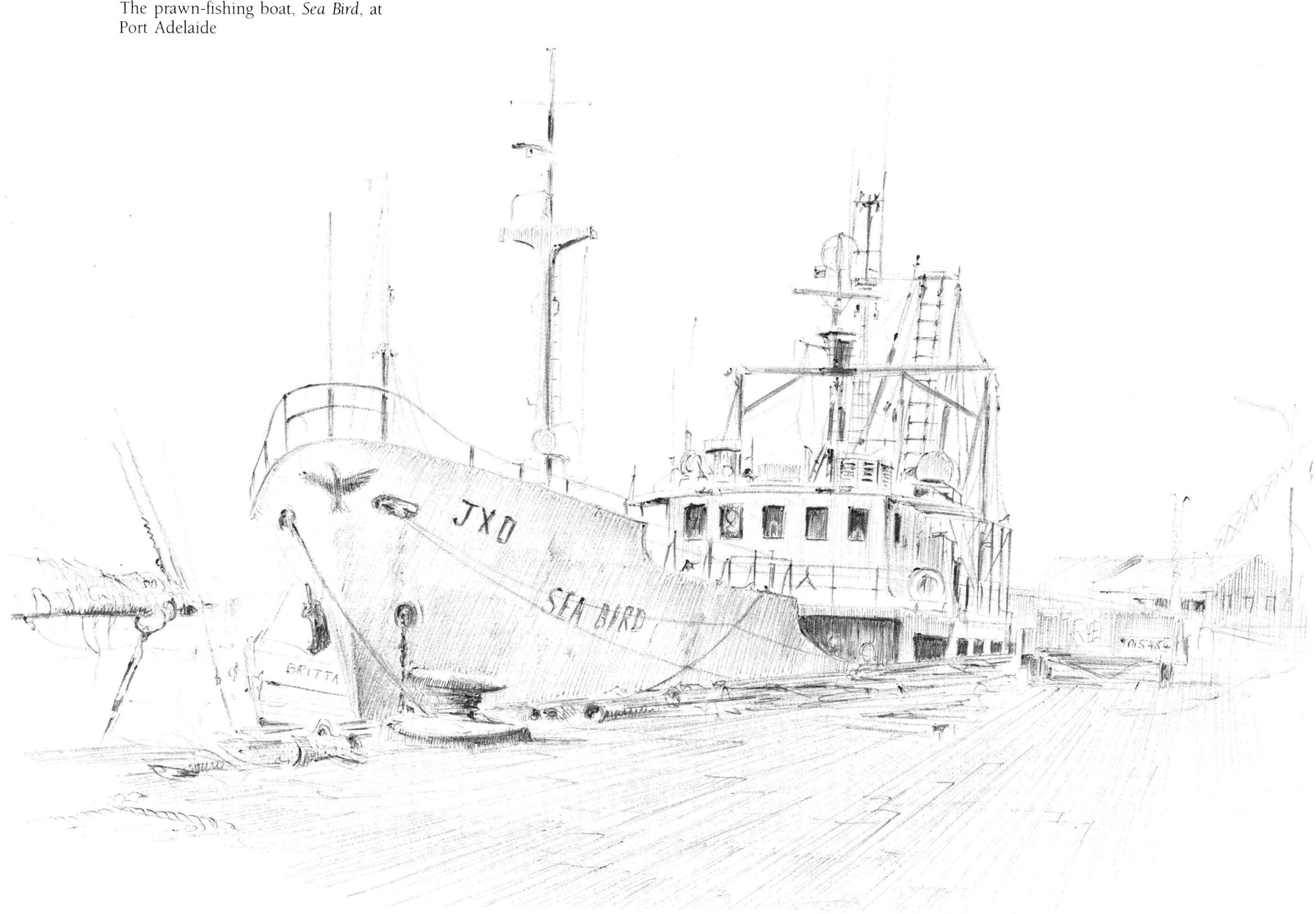

The prawn-fishing boat, *Sea Bird*, at
Port Adelaide

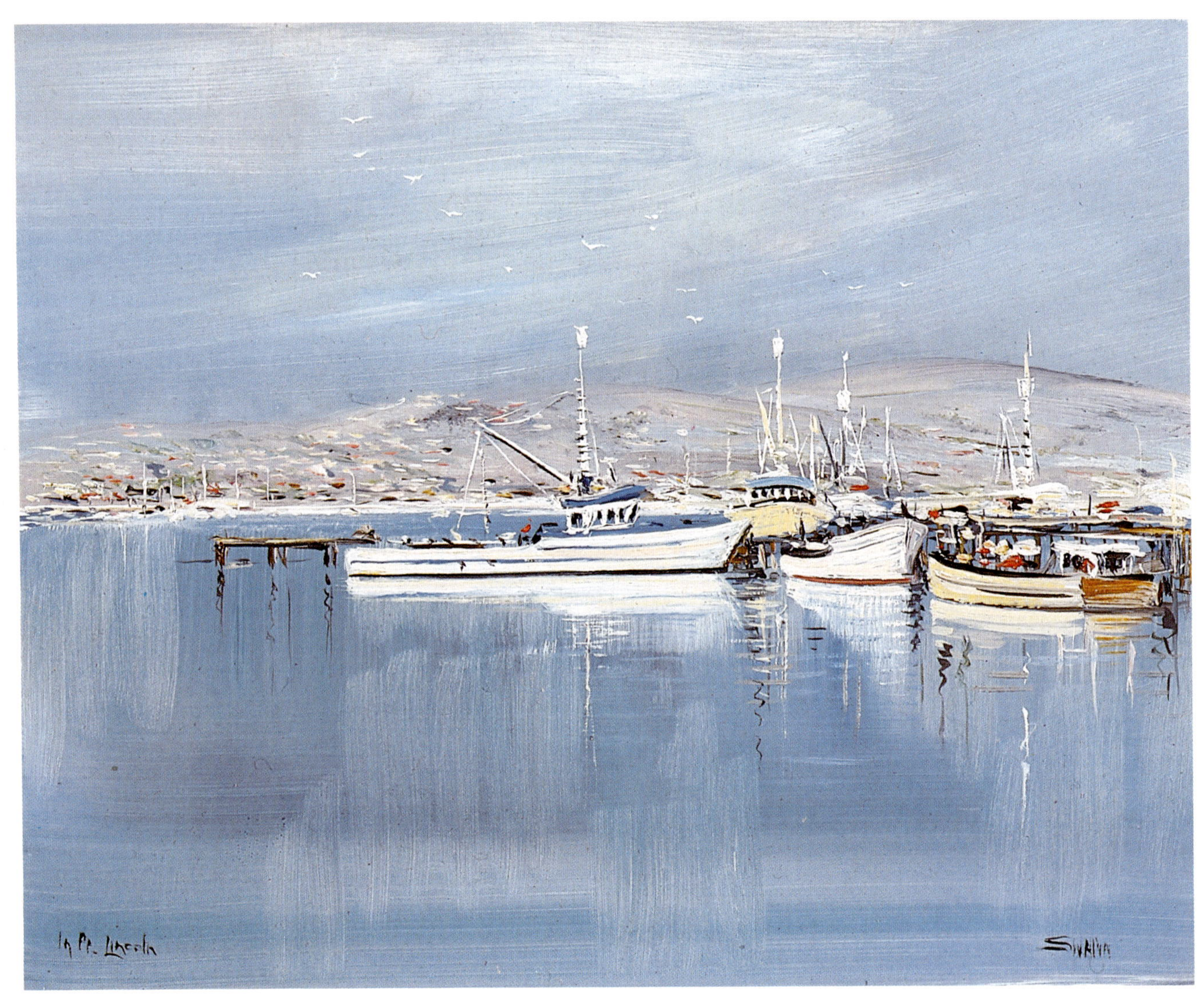

Tuna boats at Port Lincoln

*One of the prettiest and safest ports in
Australia.*

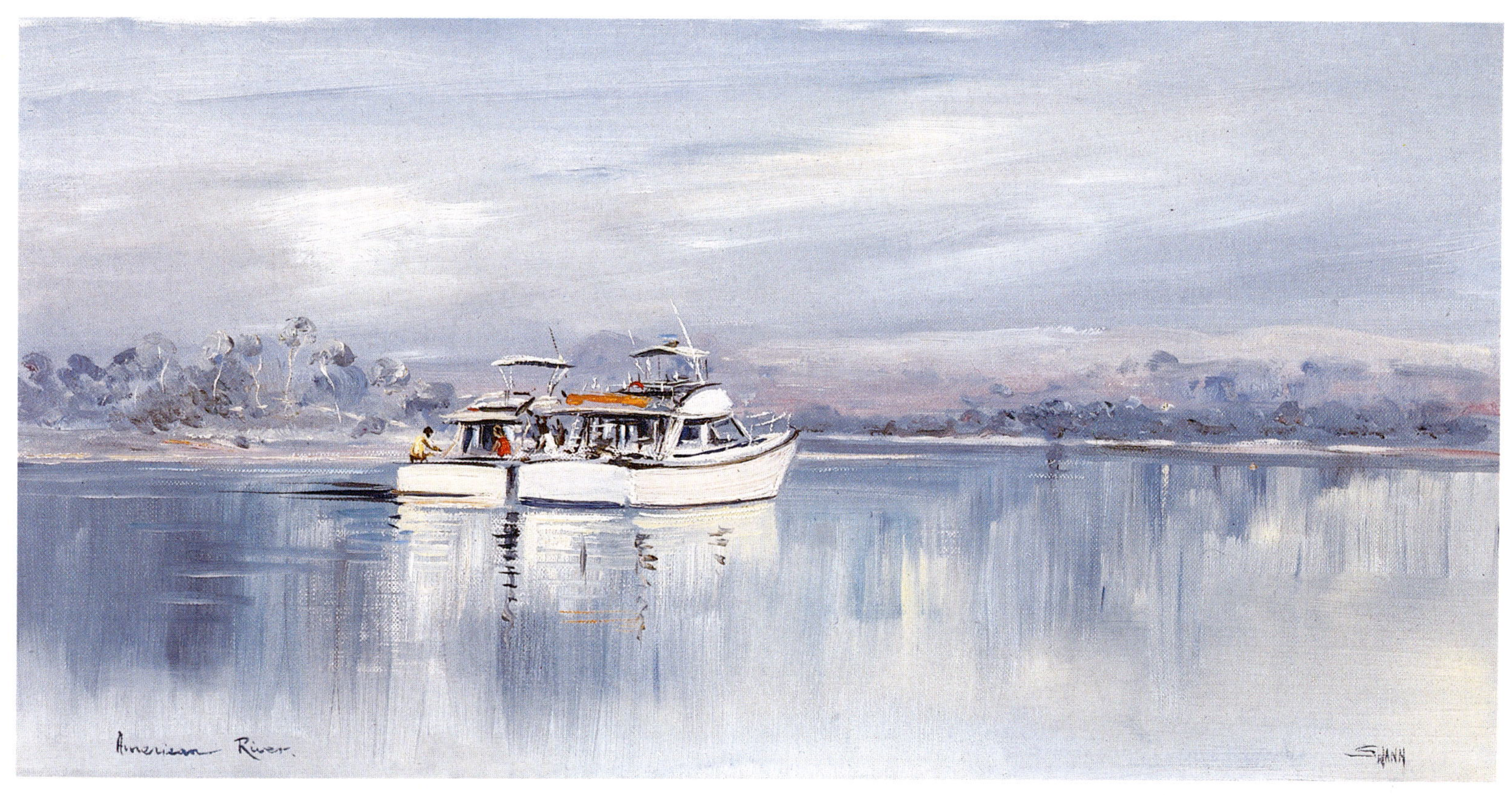

American River, Kangaroo Island

*A good spot for yachtsmen and anglers. At
the entrance of the river we had just caught a
feast of crabs.*

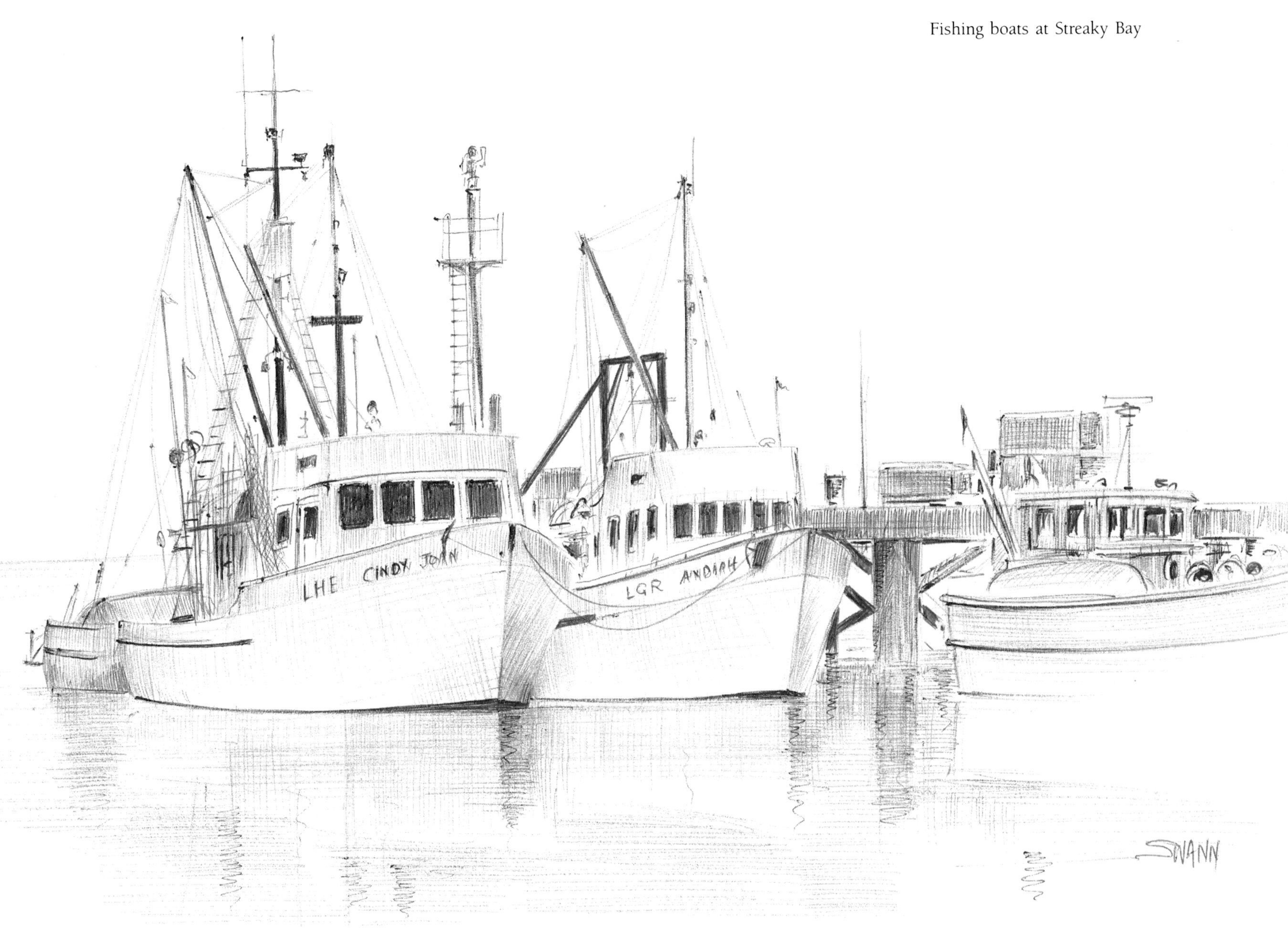

Fishing boats at Streaky Bay

The Royal South Australian Yacht
Squadron

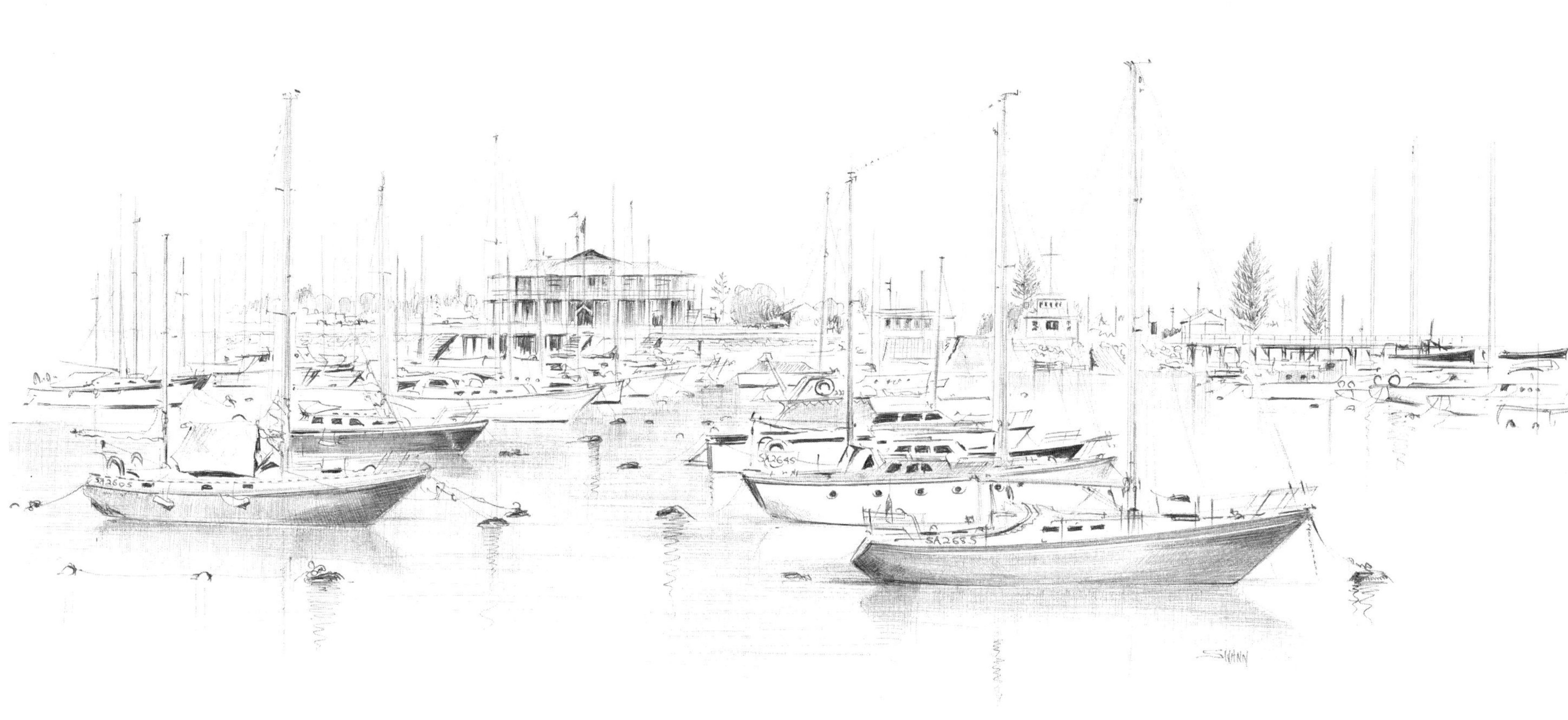

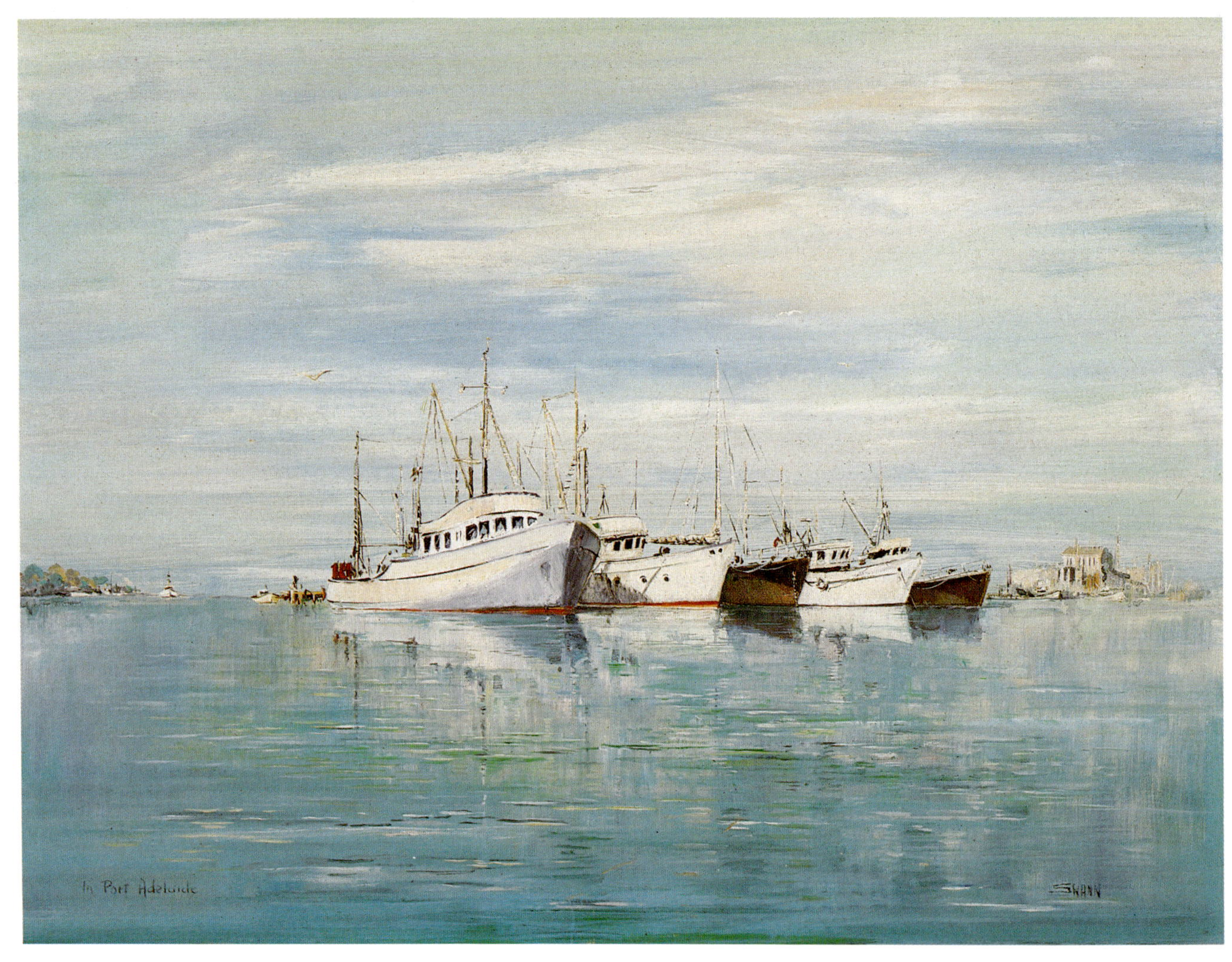

Prawn-fishing boats at rest in the
north arm of the Port River

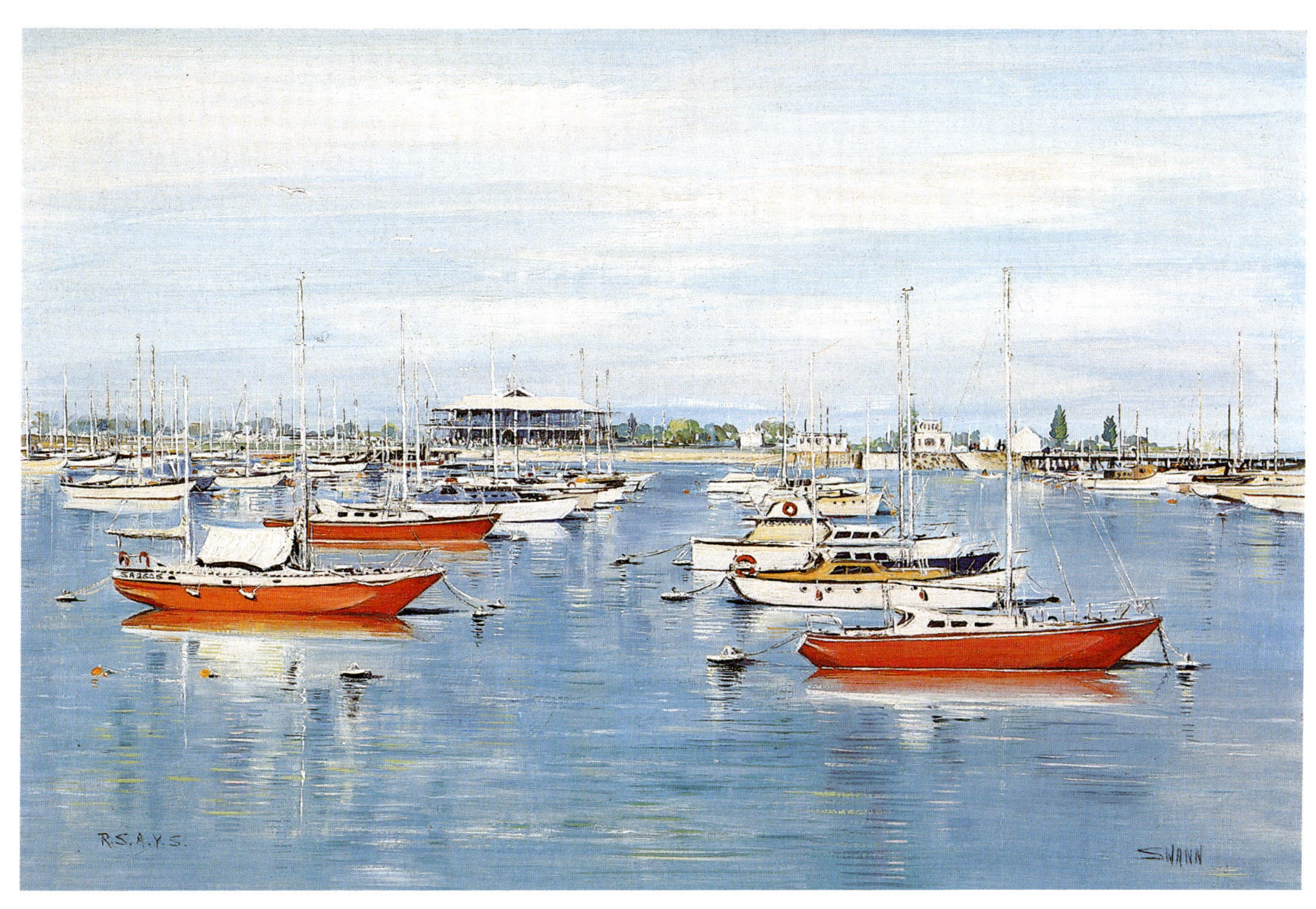

The Royal South Australian Yacht
Squadron

Department of Marine and Harbour
moorings at Port Adelaide

*Work boats and a fisheries research boat tied
up in The Creek.*

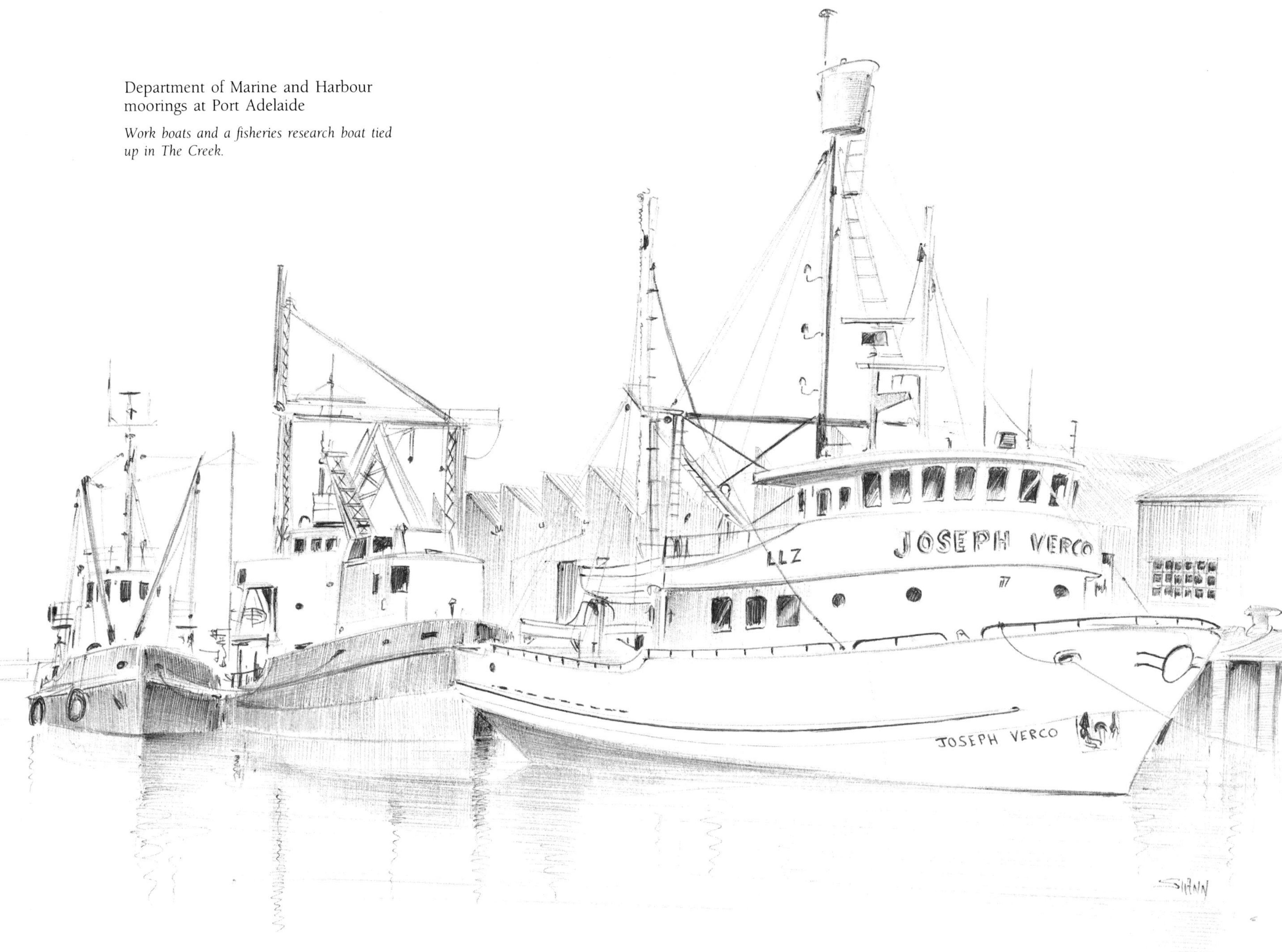

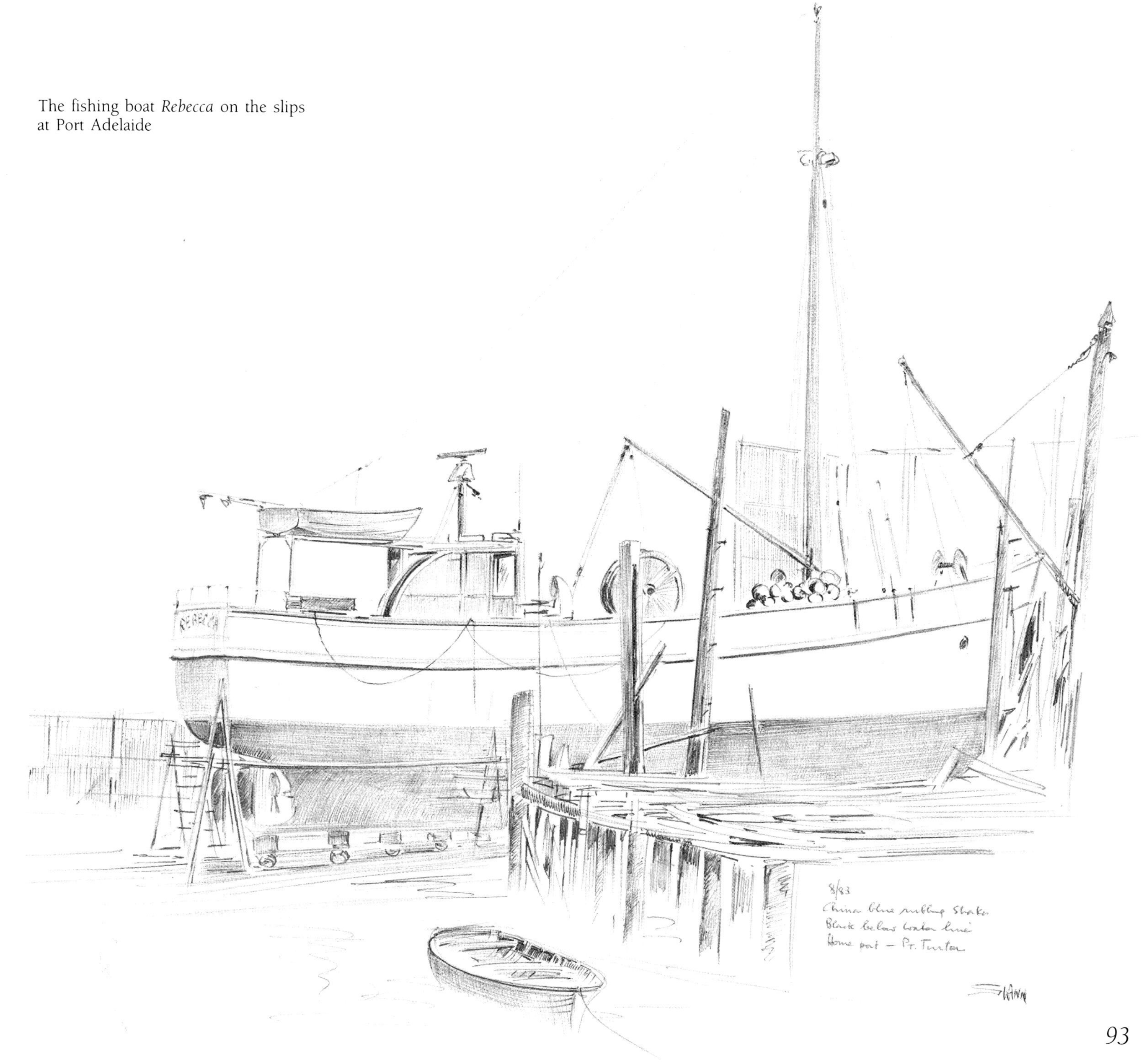

The fishing boat *Rebecca* on the slips
at Port Adelaide

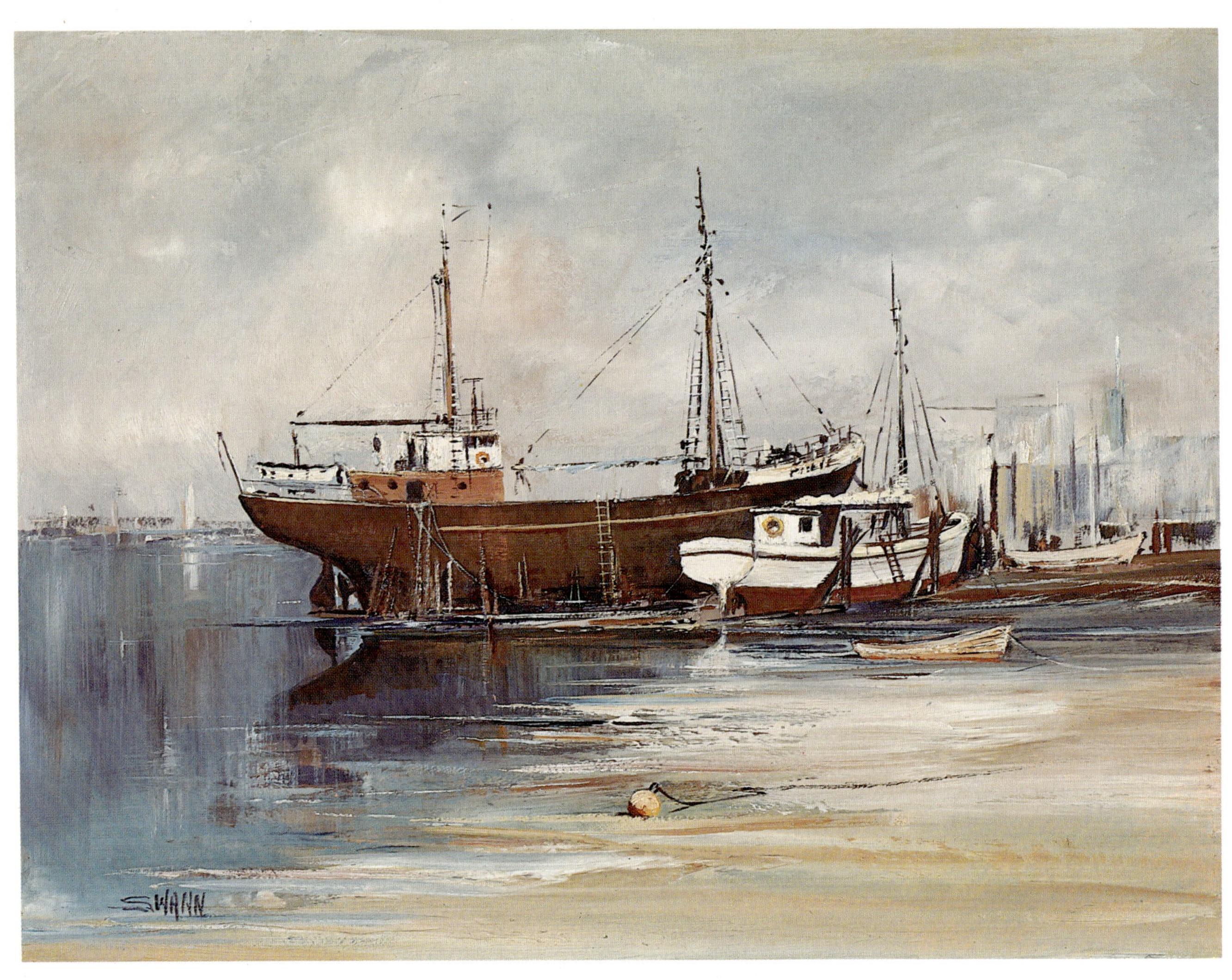

The *Falie* on the slips in 1978

*This ketch has recently been restored as a
project for South Australia's Jubilee 150.*

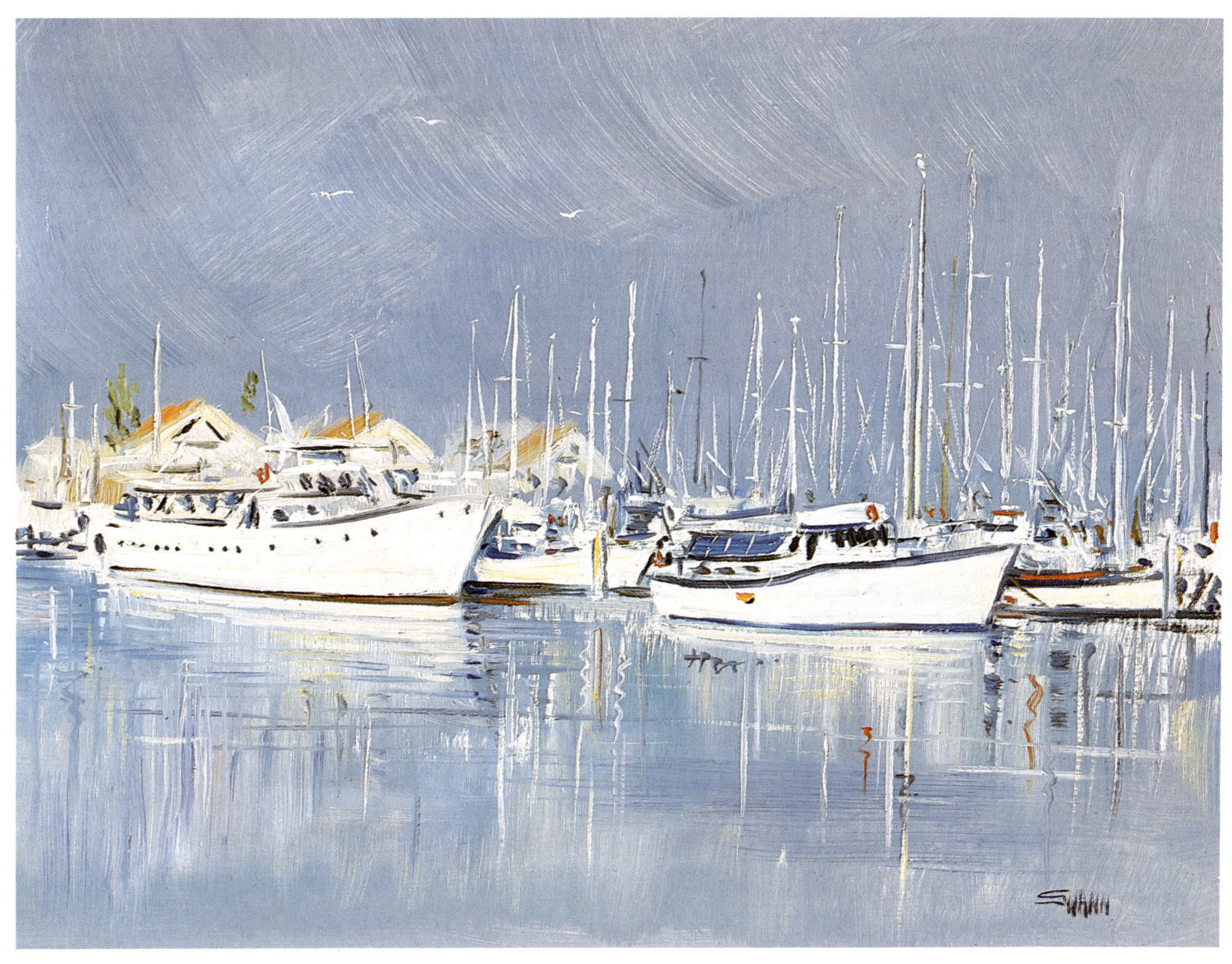

The Cruising Yacht Club of South
Australia

*The new marina, complete with towering
masts, guilded transoms, sleek white hulls and
a welter of rigging.*

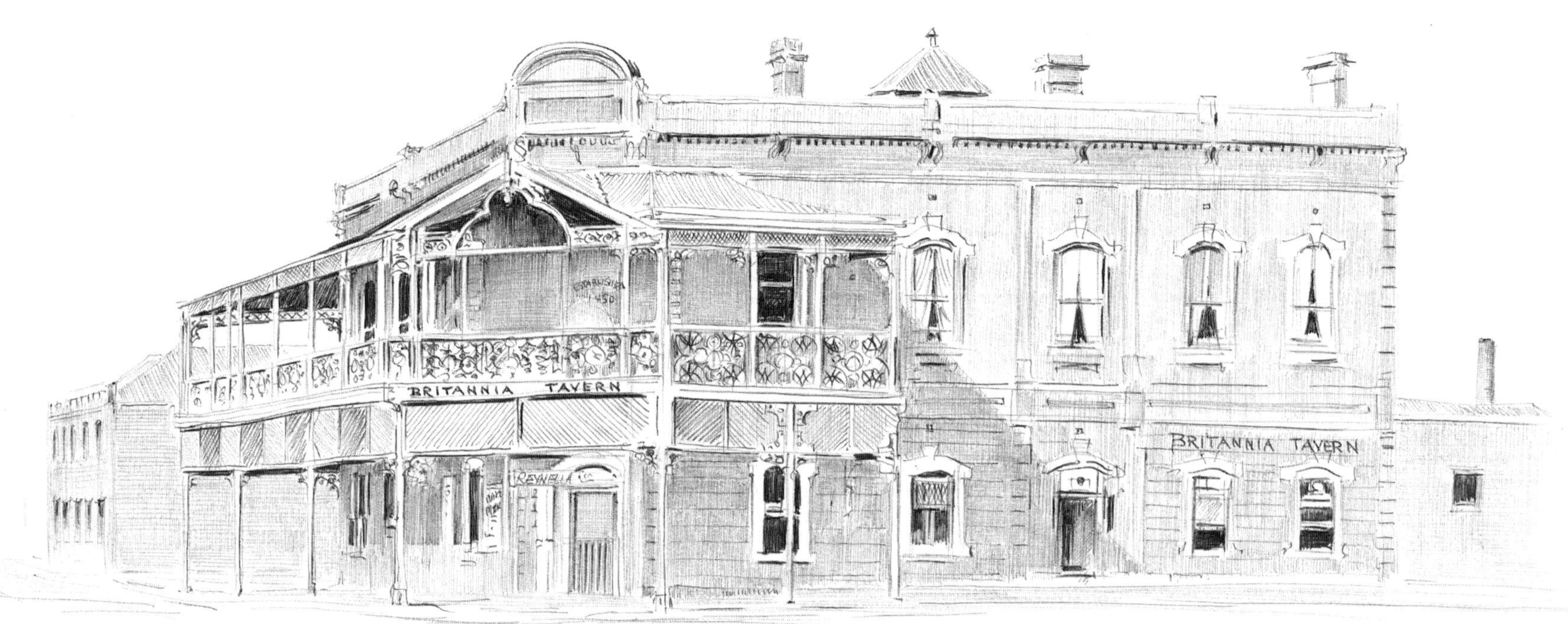

The Britannia Tavern, Port Adelaide

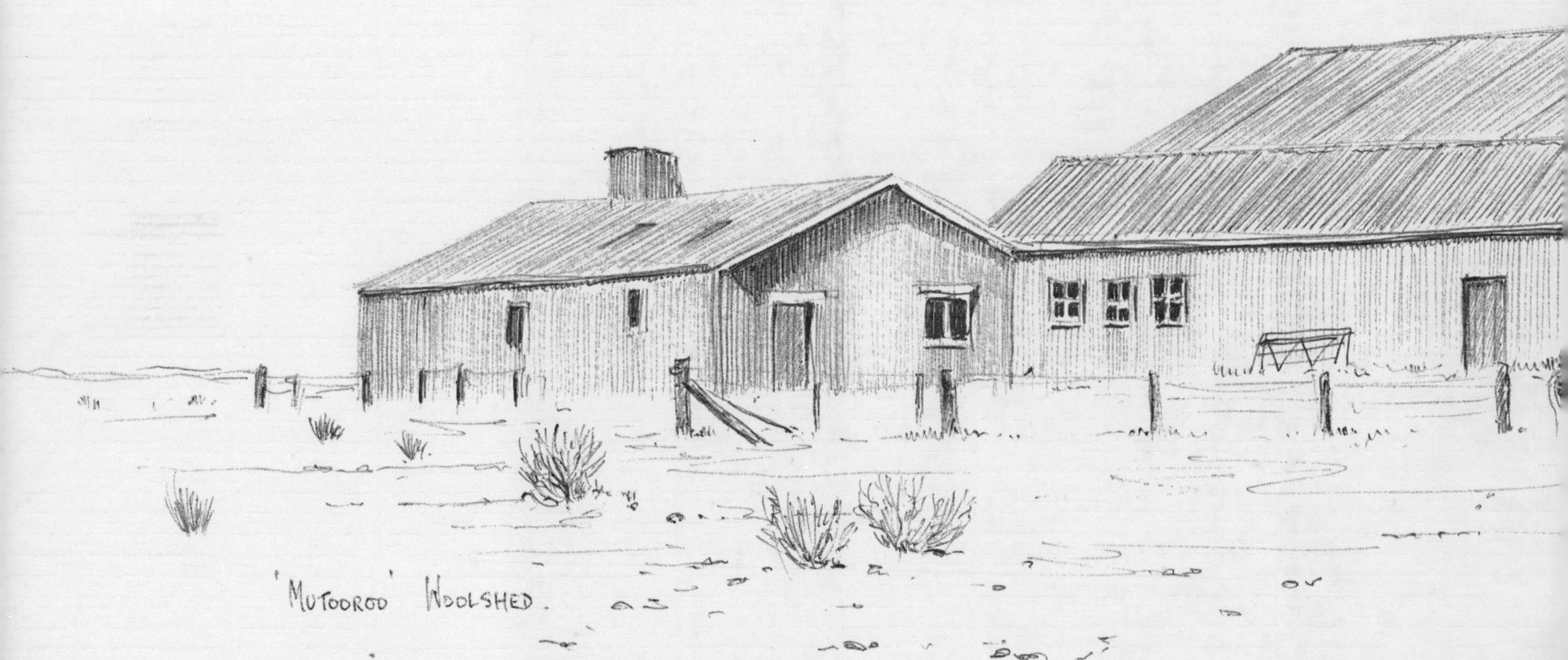

'MUTOOROO' WOOLSHED.